The World of
Rembrandt

TIME-LIFE LIBRARY OF ART

The World of Rembrandt

1606 - 1669

by Robert Wallace
and
the Editors of TIME-LIFE BOOKS

TIME-LIFE INTERNATIONAL (NEDERLAND) N.V.

About the Author

Robert Wallace has published more than 100 nonfiction articles as well as numerous short stories and poems. His first writing on art was for LIFE's series "The History of Western Culture," to which he contributed an article on the Renaissance. He is the author of *Rise of Russia* for TIME-LIFE BOOKS' Great Ages of Man series and a previous Library of Art volume, *The World of Leonardo,* the fruit of more than a year's intensive study in European and American museums and libraries. Having examined the art of great historical epochs, Mr. Wallace will move into the modern era with *The World of Van Gogh,* a forthcoming Library of Art subject.

The Consulting Editor

H. W. Janson is Professor of Fine Arts at New York University, where he is also Chairman of the Department of Fine Arts at Washington Square College. Among his numerous publications are his *History of Art* and *The Sculpture of Donatello.*

The Consultant for This Book

Seymour Slive is Professor of Fine Arts and Chairman of the Department of Fine Arts at Harvard University. He has also taught at Oberlin College and Pomona College and has been an exchange professor at the University of Leningrad. He was a Fulbright Research Scholar, the recipient of a Guggenheim Fellowship, and has been honored by the Dutch government as an Officer of the Order of the House of Orange-Nassau for his work on a Frans Hals exhibition in Haarlem in 1962. Dr. Slive is the author of numerous books and articles on 17th Century Dutch painting. In 1965 he made art news headlines with his discovery of a previously unknown Rembrandt painting, now in the Fogg Art Museum at Harvard.

On the Cover

Rembrandt faced himself without pretension in this self-portrait of his mid-50s. This is a detail; the full painting is shown on page 13.

End Papers

Rembrandt frequently walked and sketched along the banks of the Amstel River. Front: *The Bend in the Amstel River with Kostveloren Castle and Two Men on Horseback,* c. 1650-1652. Back: *The Amsteldijk near the Trompenburg Estate,* c. 1650. By permission of the Trustees of the Chatsworth Settlement, England.

Contents

An Autobiography without Words

No artist has left a loftier or more penetrating personal testament than Rembrandt van Rijn. In more than 90 portraits of himself that date from the outset of his career in the 1620s to the year of his death in 1669, he created an autobiography in art that is the equal of the finest ever produced in literature—even of the intimately analytical *Confessions* of St. Augustine.

As a young man Rembrandt probably had no thought of addressing himself to future centuries through his self-portraits. Often, like an actor practicing before a mirror, he sought simply to increase his mastery of facial expression—as seen in the greatly enlarged etching opposite, in which he registered horror or alarm. (The etching is reproduced in its actual size on the following page.) However, as Rembrandt aged and experienced the reality of emotion instead of merely studying its surface signs, he used his face to convey a deeper meaning, pitilessly portraying the slow ruin of his own flesh, reflecting the tides of skepticism and courage, melancholy and calm that coursed through him. In so doing he captured the universal, describing not only his pilgrimage but also that of all humanity toward a final peace with this world and with God.

Rembrandt was homely, and he knew it. He seems to have relished that fact when in 1630, at 24, he made the small etchings above (shown in their actual size), in which he experimented with various expressions. He appears also to have been an "angry young man,"

Self-Portrait as a Young Man, 1629

challenging a society that had not yet given him acclaim.

The oil painting above, also reproduced in its actual measurements, shows Rembrandt at 23. The bold aspect of his character appears both in his expression and in the accents vigorously scored into his hair with the butt end of his brush. But he had another aspect: a romantic as well as a realist, he loved to dress in rich costumes and dream of other realms. On the following pages he appears as a wealthy grandee and as a cavalier in flamboyant revels with his bride.

9

Self-Portrait in an Oriental Costume with a Dog, 1631

Self-Portrait with Saskia, c. 1635

11

It would be presumptuous to read a left-to-right narrative into this group of Rembrandt's self-portraits, but at least his circumstances at the times they were produced—from his 34th year to about his 54th—can be set forth. In 1640 he is the most successful artist in Amsterdam. Ten years later his wife is dead, and his popularity is fading. In 1652 he seems to sense his oncoming bankruptcy. The self-portrait of about 1657 (*directly below*) shows him after this disaster, pained and weary, but in 1658 he sees himself as ennobled and calm. In the next picture, an oil sketch, he appears to be relating his own experience to the vulnerability of all mankind. Yet around the same time, in the last of these paintings, he could celebrate man's majestic capacity to survive and to continue his struggle.

Self-Portrait, 1640

Small Self-Portrait, 1656-1658

Self-Portrait of 1658

Self-Portrait, 1650

Large Self-Portrait, 1652

Self-Portrait, Study, c. 1660

Self-Portrait, c. 1660

13

16

of contemporary biographers are few and in several instances misleading. The first treatment of Rembrandt, which appeared in 1641 as part of a history of his birthplace, the town of Leiden, was written by a onetime burgomaster, Jan Orlers. Nothing in Orlers' work has been found to be inaccurate, but it covers less than half of Rembrandt's artistic career— his early years—and is only a few hundred words in length. In 1675, six years after Rembrandt's death, Joachim von Sandrart, a German artist who had known him, produced a memoir of about 800 words. These two meager accounts, plus some observations in the autobiography of the Dutch scholar-statesman Constantin Huygens, constitute almost the entire body of material written by men who had first-hand knowledge of Rembrandt.

In 1686 an Italian churchman and art historian, Filippo Baldinucci, who obtained his information from one of Rembrandt's pupils, published a brief commentary about him as part of a volume dealing with many graphic artists. It was not until 1718, nearly a half-century after Rembrandt's death, that the first full-dress biography appeared—and even that is very slim by modern standards. Written by Arnold Houbraken, whose *De Groote Schouburgh der Nederlantsche Kunstschilders* (Great Theater of Netherlandish Artists) remains the best source-book on Dutch artists of the period, it contains valuable comments on Rembrandt's work as it was then viewed. In areas outside art, however, it has proved as vulnerable as earlier accounts. Sandrart had implanted the legend that Rembrandt was an ignoramus who "could but poorly read Netherlandish and hence profit but little from books." Baldinucci left the misinformation that Rembrandt worked for the court of Sweden. When it was Houbraken's turn to set down the facts, he mislocated the artist's birthplace, added five years to his life and noted that he was an only son (Rembrandt had four brothers).

It may appear picayune to dwell on these errors, but they make it difficult not to raise an eyebrow at some of the tales Houbraken supplies when he sets out to describe Rembrandt as a man. Houbraken says, for example, that Rembrandt was a miserly soul whose avarice was such that "his pupils, who noticed this, often for fun would paint on the floor or elsewhere, where he was bound to pass, pennies, two-penny pieces and shillings . . . after which he frequently stretched out his hand in vain, without letting anything be noticed as he was embarrassed through his mistake." The biographer also reports that Rembrandt, who willfully broke all the "rules," once "painted a picture in which the colors were so heavily loaded that you could lift it from the floor by the nose." Other stories, however, are not so easy to reject. There is some evidence that Rembrandt was at times irascible and whimsical. According to Houbraken, "One day he was working on a great portrait group in which man and wife and children were to be seen. When he had half completed it, his [Rembrandt's] monkey happened to die. As he had no other canvas available at the moment, he portrayed the dead ape in the aforesaid picture. Naturally the people concerned would not tolerate the disgusting dead ape alongside of them in the picture. But no: He so adored the model offered by the dead ape that he would rather keep the unfinished picture than obliterate the ape in order to please the people portrayed by him." Possibly the tale is true; Rembrandt was a man of highly independent mind, delighted in drawing and painting animals, and may have thought the dead monkey more interesting than the particular family he was dealing with.

The relative lack of accurate contemporary accounts of Rembrandt is not the result of carelessness or loss through the centuries, nor is it because he was not widely known and admired during his lifetime; he was. The difficulty stems in large part from the temperament of the Dutch people, who have never been at ease in the world of reflective or descriptive prose. They take the view that a painting is to be looked at, beer is to be drunk and life is to be lived—without the aid of a tedious libretto. With one or two notable exceptions, the Dutch have not produced poets, playwrights, novelists, letter-writers or critics of the first rank. They prefer to act and wordlessly to contemplate, not to involve themselves in comment or analysis, and thus during the golden century of their art they made only sparse notes about their greatest painters.

This reticence in prose had its counterpart in art. During Rembrandt's lifetime the Dutch people, numbering fewer than three million, accomplished prodigies. They threw off the yoke of Spain and established an independent nation. On the sea they challenged England and for a time forced that great maritime power into second place. The Channel and the North Sea, the green, rich Indies of the East and West heard the thunder of their cannon and saw the triumph of their flag. But Dutch artists rarely glorified such things; instead they perfected the still life.

Fortunately the advanced research techniques of modern scholars, spurred by the commemoration in 1969 of the 300th anniversary of Rembrandt's death, have made it possible to extract a good deal of new information from the silent past and to correct errors made in the intervening centuries. Sandrart's view of Rembrandt as a semi-literate has been demolished, and so too—at least among students of art history—has been the notion that the *Night Watch* marked a sudden, dramatic downturn in Rembrandt's fortunes. It is now known that the artist never went to Sweden, nor did he, as other old legends insist, reside for a time in England or travel in Italy. Thus, even if frequently through the correction of mistakes, the store of knowledge about him has been considerably increased. In relation to the remarkable breadth and depth of Rembrandt's art it is fascinating to find, at long last, that he may never have left his homeland; indeed, that he probably passed his entire life within a radius of only a few score miles. All his voyaging was done on the inward sea of his own spirit.

In any case the real measure of Rembrandt is to be found in his works, and even a hasty glance at them reveals much that is not included in his myth. Although he is commonly associated with only a half-dozen paintings—*The Anatomy Lesson of Dr. Tulp*, the *Night Watch, The Syndics of the Drapers' Guild*, the *Aristotle and Homer*, and two or three self-portraits—he was, in fact, one of the most productive artists the world has known. As many as 2,300 of his works survive and have thus far been identified—some 600 paintings, 1,400 drawings and 300 etchings.

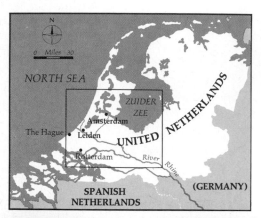

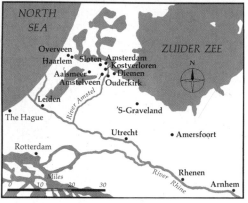

Rembrandt never traveled farther than 60 miles from Amsterdam, passing his entire life within the area shown in the box on the top map above. Leiden, his birthplace; Amsterdam, where he worked; and towns he visited are indicated in bold type on the lower map. Although for years scholars assumed that he had also visited Italy, Sweden and England—partly because some of his landscapes resembled far-off locales— his favorite scenery lay just outside Amsterdam. Along the banks of the Amstel River, he sketched the tidy hamlets and sturdy windmills *(pages 97-100)* that still dot the flat countryside.

It is possible that still others will come to light in our time. One recent identification of one of his paintings was made only in 1962. Although it is not a great work of art, it has considerable importance because it is Rembrandt's earliest known dated painting. Executed on a wooden panel, it depicts his version of the martyrdom by stoning of St. Stephen *(pages 26-27)*. Long the property of the museum of Lyons in France, it was attributed vaguely to "the school of Rembrandt" and relegated to a storeroom until two Dutch scholars, suspecting its true authorship, suggested that a corner of it be cleaned. A few swipes of the swab revealed the undoubted monogram of the master and the date, 1625, when he was only 18 or 19.

Although there is a possibility that some Rembrandt drawings, or even a cache of them, will turn up one day in an old chest or bureau drawer, the likelihood of a major discovery is not great. Collectors and connoisseurs have apparently exhausted the field. However, single drawings are still occasionally found. The task of firmly attributing a drawing to Rembrandt is by no means easy; he was a prodigiously active draftsman who rarely signed his small sketches and used whatever paper he happened to find handy, including printed pages, the backs of bills and even of funeral announcements. Most of his drawings can be identified only on stylistic grounds, and in this area scholars are not in unanimous agreement.

Among the 2,300 works there are at least 90 self-portraits—60 of them paintings and the rest etchings and drawings. In addition, Rembrandt's face appears in at least five other works as that of a spectator or participant in the action. No other great artist is known to have represented himself so frequently, which suggests a well-developed vanity on his part—until the portraits are studied. Although there were occasions in his young manhood when he may have wished to appear handsomer than he was, and although he sometimes used his own face merely as a model, contorting it into expressions of anger, joy or shock, he took, in general, a very penetrating, even merciless view of himself. Rembrandt's overriding artistic concern was with the human spirit or, in a phrase that appears in one of his letters, with expressing "the greatest inward emotion." In his quest for an understanding of mankind he found it necessary to begin with self-searching; in the visual arts no one has more closely followed the ancient Greek dictum, "Know thyself," with all the courage that such a seemingly simple injunction demands. A moving spiritual autobiography can be extracted from his self-portraits, but it is best to turn first to the physical events of his early life.

Rembrandt Harmenszoon van Rijn was born in Leiden, about 25 miles south of Amsterdam, on the 15th of July, 1606. His father, Harmen, was a miller whose surname, van Rijn, indicates that the family had lived for some generations beside or near the Rhine River. His mother, Cornelia (or Neeltgen) Willemsdochter van Zuytbrouck, was a baker's daughter. Traditionally their large family—Rembrandt was the eighth of nine children—has been described as poor and struggling. The artist's vitality and his almost ferocious energy, some critics suggest, derived from his "peasant" background and his desire to rise above it. However, there is no evidence that the van Rijns were impoverished potato-eaters.

A 17th Century view of the section of Leiden where Rembrandt's family lived shows two windmills overlooking the Rhine River. The lower one was used by the artist's father and grandfather to grind corn, and Rembrandt himself may have been born in one of the buildings behind the mills.

Such "aerial" perspectives were produced by talented map-makers who combined hundreds of measurements taken on the ground with sheer cartographic guesswork.

When Rembrandt's mother died in 1640 she left an estate valued at some 10,000 florins. The precise value of that currency is very difficult to calculate now, but it is known that the wage of a 17th Century Dutch craftsman—a weaver, for example—was only three or four florins for a 12-hour day. Thus it appears that the family was fairly well-off. In some of his early self-portraits Rembrandt chose to represent himself as a beggar and as a young rebel who appeared to have a grudge against the world; his face was wide, with small eyes, a broad nose and powerful jaw. But these are not necessarily the features of a country clod, and if Rembrandt had some quarrel with the world it may have been rooted in his anger at the inhumanity of man rather than in his family circumstances.

Rembrandt's birth coincided closely with that of the Dutch nation. For generations the 17 provinces of the Low Countries (the Netherlands, Belgium and Luxembourg) had been under the rule of Catholic Spain. However in 1609, when Rembrandt was three, the seven northern provinces, under the leadership of the noble House of Orange, finally achieved the freedom for which they had been struggling for 40 years. Spain did not formally recognize their independence, but in fact the Spanish were seldom again a serious menace to Dutch liberty. The United Provinces, as the nation was then called, included Holland, Zeeland, Utrecht, Guelderland, Overijssel, Friesland and Groningen. Of these, Holland was the wealthiest and most populous—and for that reason its name was frequently used by foreigners to refer to the whole country, to the annoyance of the citizens of the other six provinces.

In the Low Countries during Rembrandt's time paintings were routinely offered for sale at country fairs. This detail from a contemporary painting by David Vinckboons shows a picture stall flanked by two other booths where clothes, pottery and musical instruments are being hawked. Artists could thus offer their wares directly to the public rather than depend solely on the relatively rare wealthy patron. Ordinary fairgoers, in turn, could afford to own a number of original paintings—some now priceless—by spending only a few florins.

The new nation was democratic in its institutions and vigilant in safeguarding them. The House of Orange, however successful it had been in rallying and leading the people, was unable to form a strong central government. The various provinces sent representatives to the modest court at The Hague, but each province regarded itself as autonomous in all matters save defense and foreign policy.

In this loose federation, the two traditional sources of patronage for artists were no longer available. During the first decades of their freedom the egalitarian Dutch cared little for titles and the courtly life, and although the House of Orange did commission works of art (including at least seven paintings by Rembrandt), aristocratic patronage was negligible. The other source of patronage, the Catholic Church, was also shut off. While Catholics still formed a sizable segment of the population when the United Provinces came into being, gradually they were submerged in the rising tide of Protestantism, particularly Calvinism. More and more, the Catholic faithful were compelled to worship in private; their churches were stripped of their altars and often were taken over for use by Protestants. In these circumstances, the Church could no longer supply the rich commissions that had nourished artists since the beginning of the Renaissance.

Thus, for the first time in history, painters assumed the independent but precarious position in society that they still occupy. Fortunately for 17th Century Dutch artists, of whom there were literally thousands, the ordinary citizens of the country replaced the Church and the aristocracy as purchasers of paintings. (Sculpture never became a major art form among the Dutch. There is no facile explanation for this; perhaps it was because monumental sculpture seemed out of place in the comfortable decor of a middle-class home, or perhaps it was because the solid burgher, who might pay a fair sum for a canvas, found his sense of propriety offended by the notion of something so grandiose, and reminiscent of "popish" church art, as a statue.)

The extent to which the average Dutchman participated in the art market is almost beyond belief. If a rough parallel may be drawn, the situation will be comparable when every second family in the United States possesses an original painting. As to why the Dutch were so fascinated by art, there is again no ready explanation. This was simply the particular form of creativity that appealed to them and for which they had enormous talent. To be sure, the typical citizen was inclined to regard painting merely as wall decoration, and his taste tended strongly to an almost photographic naturalism in portraits and scenes of everyday life, but he bought canvases in remarkable quantity. The English traveler Peter Mundy, who visited Amsterdam in 1640, noted with some astonishment that "As For the art off Painting and the affection off the people to Pictures, I thincke none other goe beeyond them there having been in this Country Many excellent Men in thatt Facullty, some att present, as Rimbrantt, etts., All in general striving to adorne their houses, especially the outer or street roome, with costly peeces, Butchers and bakers not much inferior in their shoppes, which are Fairely sett Forth, yea many tymes blacksmithes, Coblers, etts., will have some picture or other by their Forge and in their stalle. . . ."

In such a climate it was natural for artists to be extremely productive. If it can be believed, it is recorded that Michiel van Miereveld, an able Utrecht painter, produced more than 10,000 portraits in his career. Miereveld lived to be 74, and if he began painting at 14 and continued for 60 years, his output averaged better than three portraits a week. It is also recorded that Cornelis Ketel, another good artist, who apparently became bored with the endless turning out of portraits, used to amuse himself and his clients by painting with his toes.

A s may be suggested by Miereveld's and Ketel's activities, the Dutch artist of the 17th Century was frank to acknowledge himself as a craftsman, a producer of goods. Although such masters of the High Renaissance as Leonardo and Michelangelo had made it very plain, in the Italy of the preceding century, that art was no mechanical exercise but the loftiest of callings, Dutch painters had little of that sentiment. In general they accepted their fairly humble status (Rembrandt took exception to this) and asked no special deference. As a rule they did not feel called upon, as had the Italians, to write argumentative treatises to explain themselves and their theories—and therein lies still another reason for the sparseness of knowledge about them.

Despite the vigor of the art market, exceedingly few Dutch painters prospered and died rich. An oversupply of paintings depressed prices, with the result that a good canvas sometimes sold for as little as 10 or 15 florins. Rembrandt, at the height of his popularity, received the resoundingly handsome sum of 1,600 florins for the *Night Watch,* and later

Still standing in the heart of Rotterdam, this life-size bronze representation of the Netherlands' foremost scholar, the great humanist Desiderius Erasmus, by the sculptor Hendrik de Keyser, was the only public statue erected in the Dutch Republic in the 17th Century—a rarity that may have been due in part to a democratic aversion to hero worship.

became bankrupt not through lack of good commissions but through mismanagement of his affairs. But other fine artists were forced to become tavernkeepers or ferrymen in order to make ends meet. It is said that Hercules Seghers, whose romantic scenes influenced Rembrandt's landscapes, withdrew from the struggle and died an alcoholic. Frans Hals and Meindert Hobbema had grim financial problems. Jan Vermeer at the time of his death owed a baker's bill of 617 florins, for which the baker (no doubt grudgingly) was obliged to accept two paintings—their identity since lost—that might have made his descendants incalculably rich.

Rembrandt's decision to become an artist, or perhaps more accurately his parents' decision to establish him in such a chancy career, was not taken early. As a boy he must have impressed his parents as the most promising of their children—of their other sons who survived to manhood, one became first a cobbler and then a miller, and another a baker—and accordingly they sent Rembrandt to the Latin School in Leiden to prepare him for a learned profession. In the United Provinces it was not unthinkable that a miller's son could aspire to any position, however high, and his parents evidently knew the value of an education. Among Rembrandt's drawings there is one which shows a small family group, probably his own, seated around a book on a candlelit table. His mother, whom he often portrayed with a Bible on her knees and who several times served as a model in his Biblical paintings, was a devout reader of Scripture; doubtless he first absorbed from her the sense of God, man and nature that was to make him the most profoundly Christian of all Protestant artists.

The Latin School, which Rembrandt attended from his seventh to his 14th year, placed heavy emphasis on religious studies. Its curriculum, apparently unknown to early writers who commented on Rembrandt's ignorance, also included the reading of Cicero, Terence, Virgil, Ovid, Horace, Caesar, Sallust, Livy and Aesop. The students conversed in Latin, and Rembrandt became accustomed to the Latin form of his own name, Rembrantus Harmensis Leydensis (Rembrandt the son of Harmen of Leiden). It was for this reason that he signed his early works with the monogram, RHL. Rembrandt not only passed the course, but later recalled it in detail; his historical and mythological paintings reflect meticulous attention to the texts on which they were based.

It was the purpose of the Latin School to prepare young men for admission to the University of Leiden, which in Rembrandt's time was the equal of any in Europe. The French philosopher Descartes, who wrote his *Discourse on Method* while living in the United Provinces, passed some time there, as did other scholars of his caliber. In all likelihood, Rembrandt never had much contact with such men, but he early developed an admiration for the "old philosopher" in general—a type that appears frequently in his paintings. Nor did Rembrandt pursue his formal education much beyond the Latin School; he went so far as to be matriculated in the University, but withdrew apparently after only a month or two. It was at this point, sometime in 1620, that he turned to art.

The name of Rembrandt's first teacher, mentioned only as "a painter" in old accounts, is unknown. His second, under whom he served a three-year apprenticeship, was an obscure and none-too-talented Leiden painter named Jacob van Swanenburgh, who specialized in architectural scenes and views of hell. Van Swanenburgh, like many other Dutch artists of the time, had studied in Italy but apparently had not profited much from the experience. He taught Rembrandt the fundamentals of drawing, etching and painting but does not seem to have made a deep impression on his pupil. In later years Rembrandt turned his hand to almost every subject that may occur to an artist—except architecture and hell. (Architecture appears in many of Rembrandt's backgrounds, to be sure, but unlike van Swanenburgh he never treated it *per se*.)

By the time he was 17 or 18, Rembrandt had absorbed all that van Swanenburgh could teach him and had shown such promise that his father sent him to Amsterdam to study under Pieter Lastman, who was then one of the foremost painters of historical scenes in the United Provinces. Lastman, too, had been to Italy, where he had been much impressed by the works of Caravaggio and particularly of Adam Elsheimer, a German painter who lived in Rome. The outstanding qualities of Caravaggio were a bold naturalism, dramatic power and especially an atmosphere of mysterious depth conveyed by chiaroscuro, the interplay of light and shadow. Elsheimer responded to Caravaggio's innovations, but instead of making life-size paintings as the Italian did, he specialized in small, cabinet-size, highly finished paintings with exquisite daylight and nocturnal effects. Lastman was influenced by both artists and in turn transmitted what he had learned to his own pupils. Rembrandt, who was thus indirectly a pupil of Caravaggio and Elsheimer, remained in Lastman's studio for only six months, but he quickly seized the chiaroscuro device and, within a short time, began to use it with a skill no other artist has ever surpassed.

Rembrandt's early art training included practice in the use of perspective by reference to intricate architectural studies like the one above. He quickly mastered such problems as the depiction of the winding staircase and effectively employed this complex device in the painting below, produced when he was 27. As a mature artist, Rembrandt often sketched city walls, cottages and ruins, but in his paintings architectural motifs were subordinated to his primary objective—the portrayal of human character.

From Lastman Rembrandt derived other elements of his early style—the use of bright, glossy colors and lively, sometimes theatrical gestures in paintings of fairly small scale. It was probably Lastman, too, who inspired Rembrandt to become a history painter—at a time when history painting was not notably fashionable among the Dutch. Theorists accepted the idea, as they had since the Renaissance, that there was a hierarchical order in the genres of painting. The noblest subject for the artist was the famous past, particularly the Biblical past, while portraits, scenes of everyday life, landscapes and still lifes were of secondary importance. However, the ordinary art buyer in the United Provinces paid little heed to art theory; he preferred subjects from daily life that were familiar to him, and so gave his trade to painters in the "minor" specialties. Nonetheless Rembrandt not only chose to take up history painting but dedicated himself to it with a fervor that lasted all his life. Although he eventually worked in almost all the specialties, he did not paint a commissioned portrait, so far as is known, until he had been established in his career for at least six years and did not venture seriously into landscape until he was in his late thirties. His preoccupation was always with history and above all with the Scriptures.

At 18 or 19 Rembrandt left Lastman, returned to Leiden and set himself up as an independent master. His recently discovered *Stoning of St. Stephen,* a product of that period, reveals flashes of his genius, but it also reveals what a steep road he had to travel before he could fully express it.

Sources of Inspiration

So distinctive was Rembrandt's own imprint on art that his debt to other painters is often overlooked. Yet the influences that helped shape his formative years can be traced as clearly as in the case of lesser men; even genius has its artistic ancestry.

Rembrandt's most notable forebear was Caravaggio, the Italian master who revolutionized the use of light and shadow *(pages 30-31)*, an innovation ardently pursued by an entire Dutch school of painters *(pages 32-33)* popular in Rembrandt's youth. He found another fount of ideas in the work of Adam Elsheimer, a German living in Rome who was also beholden to Caravaggio but who painted in much smaller scale, usually using copper plates and setting his mood with landscape backgrounds *(page 28)*. Rembrandt's teacher, Pieter Lastman, who studied in Italy, communicated Elsheimer's ideas to his eager pupil along with his own fondness for forceful gestures and dramatic scenes *(page 29)*.

Many of these familial elements appear in Rembrandt's earliest known dated painting, the recently discovered *Stoning of St. Stephen (opposite)*. It has Caravaggio's lighting, the small-scale details and a hint of the landscape of Elsheimer, and the multi-figured excitement of Lastman. But within a decade after painting this work at 19, Rembrandt was able to fashion a far more personal statement of his artistic ideas in the brilliant *Blinding of Samson (pages 34-35)*.

MUSÉE DES BEAUX ARTS, LYONS

Stoning of St. Stephen, 1625

Adam Elsheimer: *Tobias and the Angel*, c. 1610

Hendrick Goudt: *Tobias and the Angel*, 1613

Hercules Seghers: *Tobias and the Angel*, date unknown

Flight into Egypt, 1653

Pieter Lastman: *The Angel and Tobias and the Fish*, c. 1630

The transmission of subject matter and style from one 17th Century master to another often took place in a manner that may seem plagiaristic to the modern eye. Of the five works shown here, the earliest is the painting by Adam Elsheimer *(opposite, top)*. It illustrates an incident in the Apocryphal Book of Tobit in which Tobit's son Tobias, accompanied by an angel, captures a huge fish in the Tigris River. About 20 years later Pieter Lastman, who had been influenced by Elsheimer, still had his works in mind when he painted this theme *(above)*, although the picture is by no means a slavish imitation.

Elsheimer had other Dutch followers, among them the gifted printmaker Count Hendrick Goudt, who copied his works as exactly as possible; Goudt's engraving *(second from top, opposite)* is such a copy, with the composition reversed. After this print was circulated in Holland, the landscape artist Hercules Seghers adapted it for his own purposes *(third from top, opposite)*. Later Seghers' copper plate was purchased by Rembrandt, who burnished out the figures of Tobias and the angel and replaced them with a grouping of the Holy Family, transforming the subject into a *Flight into Egypt (bottom, opposite)*. Although Rembrandt left much of Seghers' plate intact, his alteration entirely changed the mood and meaning of the work.

Michelangelo Merisi da Caravaggio, who died in 1610, ranks
high among the masters who have given decisive impetus to
Western painting. His influence, radiating from Italy, was felt not
only in Holland but throughout Europe during his lifetime and for
generations thereafter. Among his most widely imitated
innovations was a powerful new use of chiaroscuro, the contrasting
of light and shadow, by which he unified his complex compositions
and obtained highly dramatic, naturalistic effects—as in his
Martyrdom of St. Matthew at right.

According to tradition St. Matthew was executed in Ethiopia by
order of its king, but Caravaggio chose to depict a scene that seems
to have taken place in some fantastic, allegorical realm rather than
in black Africa. At the right stands a screaming boy who might
well symbolize Panic, desperate to run but rooted to the spot in
terror. Three half-nude figures—their role is unclear, although
they may be the executioner's assistants—sprawl in the
foreground; the clothed figures at the left, some indifferent, some
appalled, may represent the world. An angel descends from heaven
to offer Matthew the palm of martyrdom.

Rembrandt, who never visited Italy and thus could not have
seen this painting, nevertheless had an excellent if indirect
knowledge of Caravaggio's work, obtained from Pieter Lastman,
other Dutch artists and possibly also from prints and drawings. He
fully captured Caravaggio's Baroque spirit; the shrieking boy in
the *Martyrdom* appears to be a precursor of Rembrandt's figure of
Delilah, in reverse, in his *Blinding of Samson (pages 34-35)*.

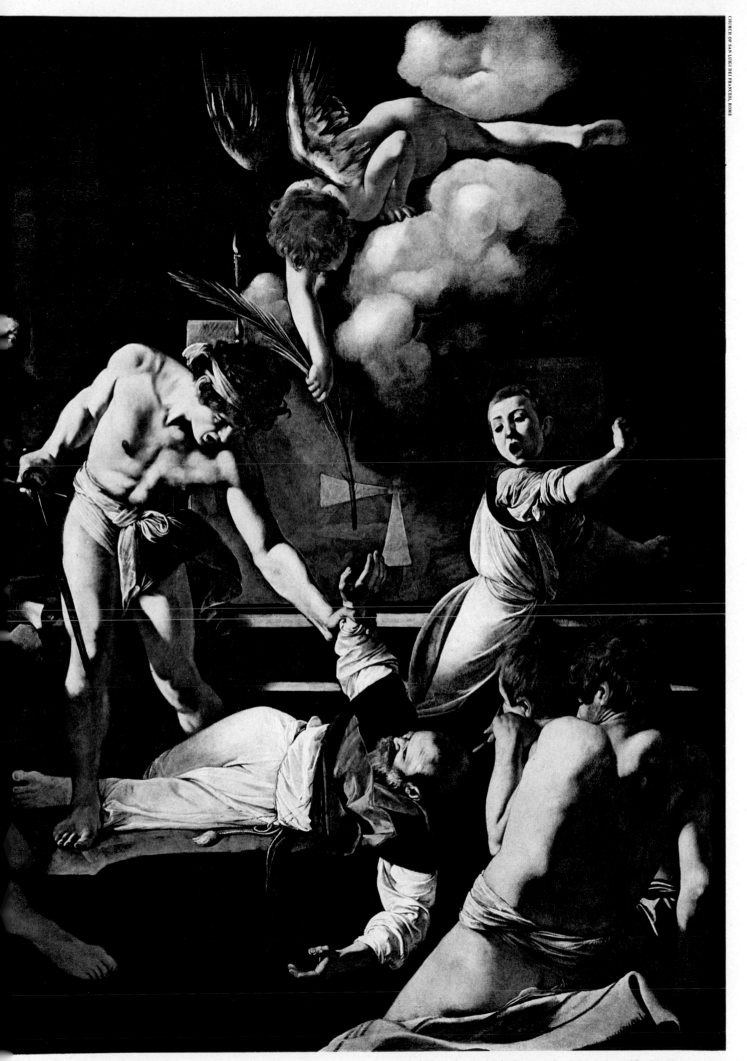

Michelangelo Merisi da Caravaggio: *Martyrdom of St. Matthew,* c. 1600

Hendrick Terbrugghen: *Young Man Lighting a Pipe from a Candle*, 1623

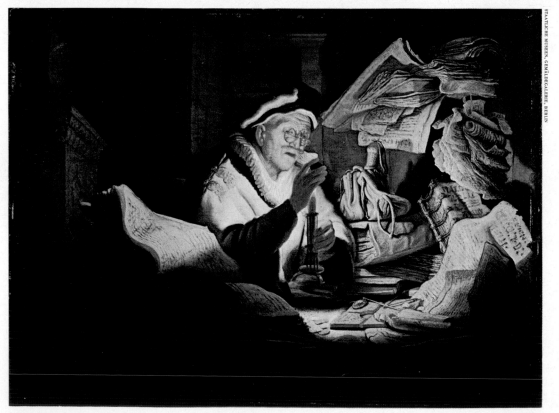

The Money Changer, 1627

Gerrit van Honthorst: *Supper Party,* 1620

Caravaggio's influence in Holland was so strong that his name has been applied to a school of Dutch painters—the Utrecht *Caravaggisti.* Among its foremost exponents were Hendrick Terbrugghen and Gerrit van Honthorst, both of whom studied his pictures in Italy, seized upon aspects of his treatment of light and shadow and exploited them in their own talented ways. In one of Terbrugghen's paintings *(above, left)* the source of light—the candle—is exposed, with the shadows presented in deep contrast. Honthorst's picture *(above)* contains a device characteristic of his paintings: the principal light source is screened from the viewer by a figure in the foreground, while the background figures are illuminated both directly and by reflection. Rembrandt must have had the opportunity to study paintings of this sort at close hand. He was intrigued by the screened light and used it with greater dramatic effect than any of his contemporaries, even in such tiny works as *The Money Changer (left),* only about 12 inches in height, which he produced at the age of 21.

33

Rembrandt's *Blinding of Samson,* the most violent of all his paintings, contains certain elements that derive from Caravaggio: the figures are large, almost life-size, and the lighting ranges from brilliance to the deepest gloom. But by the time he produced this work—in 1636, when he was 30—Rembrandt had also been influenced by Peter Paul Rubens, the Flemish master of the High Baroque. Rubens had depicted a similar moment in the Biblical story, showing the capture of Samson in a wild mêlée, but his scene included no bloodshed. Rembrandt seems to have set out to surpass Rubens by injecting a note of horror, for which there was an avid taste among contemporary viewers.

The artist's composition employs emphatic diagonals to compel the viewer's attention toward Samson's face, which is contorted in agony as a Philistine soldier plunges a long dagger into his eye. One diagonal begins at the upraised hand of Delilah *(right)* as she scurries from the scene holding the betrayed hero's shorn hair; it extends through Samson's upraised leg and the armored forearm of the soldier, and ends in the dagger-thrust. A second, stronger diagonal is achieved by the weapon of the halberdier.

Rembrandt's intent is to shock, and he succeeds mightily. But after this initial effect has diminished, it is impossible for the viewer's glance not to return to Delilah; with the mingled terror and gloating reflected on her face, she emerges as one of Rembrandt's greatest triumphs of characterization.

The Blinding of Samson, 1636

35

II

Prelude to Greatness

When Rembrandt established himself as an independent artist in Leiden, after his apprenticeship in Amsterdam, he was not yet 20. However, he was not notably precocious; his great contemporary, the Italian sculptor-architect Gianlorenzo Bernini, produced superb portrait busts in marble at the age of 13. What is remarkable in Rembrandt is the explosive speed of his development—in etching and drawing as well as in painting. In his late teens he was merely one among many talented Dutch artists, but in a half-dozen years he had surpassed almost all of them—and was still growing.

Leiden was a lively place to be in those years. How it appeared to Rembrandt's particularly perceptive eye when he returned home from Amsterdam around 1625 is impossible to tell; he made no scenes of the town—or at any rate, none that are known to survive. There are, however, a few sketches by other artists, plus some contemporary written accounts, that suggest what Rembrandt must have seen. Lying along the Old Rhine a short distance from the sea, Leiden in the 1620s had a population of about 50,000 and was second among Dutch towns only to Amsterdam (about 110,000). Architecturally it was typically Dutch. Rows of narrow houses, with gabled roofs and bright-colored shutters, leaned together beside the streets and canals. Looming above them stood the imposing ruin of a medieval castle; there had been a major settlement in Leiden at least as early as the 12th Century. The surrounding countryside was flat as a slate.

Visitors found Leiden conspicuous for its cleanliness, even in well-scrubbed Holland, but paradoxically it also had an abominable stench: its canals were almost currentless and were often clogged with rotting flotsam and sewage. Perhaps because of this the town was often racked by "plagues," a term that then included several deadly epidemic diseases; some years the death toll was so high that the cemeteries could not hold all the corpses, and many had to be buried in Leiden's earthen ramparts.

Against such calamities Leiden could measure a number of blessings. It had a great university, the first to be founded in Holland, a center of intellectual excitement. It was increasingly prosperous, both as a market

The familiar criticism of the somberness of Rembrandt's works —one contemporary labeled him an owl-like "man of darkness"—is belied by this brilliantly illumined confrontation between the blind Tobit and his wife Anna.

Tobit and Anna, 1626

37

town and as the site of a thriving textile industry, which eventually involved most of Leiden's workers. Underpaid and illiterate, they presented a sharp contrast to the professors and students at the University, among them Englishmen, Germans, Swedes, Poles and Hungarians, a number of whom came from noble families. The foreign dress of the students must have intrigued Rembrandt, who had a keen eye for such things, although in the early sketches he made from life his subjects were not wealthy young men, but the poor.

In Leiden Rembrandt worked closely with Jan Lievens, an excellent artist who was 16 months younger than he and who had also studied in Amsterdam under Pieter Lastman. From their teacher both had absorbed a clear predilection for history painting and for forceful statements that amounted at times almost to bombast; Rembrandt, in fact, would have to struggle for years to control the power in his art and to channel his innate passion and boldness away from the sensational. In the mid-1620s his style and Lievens' were remarkably similar; both used the same models and props—it is quite likely that they may have shared a studio for a time—and it sometimes requires expert knowledge to tell an early Lievens from an early Rembrandt. They probably did not go so far as to collaborate in blocking out their compositions, but it is known that they retouched each other's paintings. A note in an inventory made in 1632 of works owned by Prince Frederick Henry of Orange indicates that even their contemporaries had difficulty in distinguishing their hands. It reads: "Simeon in the Temple, holding Christ in his arms, done by Rembrandt or Jan Lievens."

One early work that is indisputably Rembrandt's is the newly identified *Stoning of St. Stephen*. If it is not an outstanding success, it nonetheless contains features that are characteristic of Rembrandt's work throughout his career. One is the use of shadow, by which he submerges the figures in the left half of the panel and thus immediately directs the attention of the viewer to the action on the right. And he creates the illusion of depth, of a series of planes that recede irregularly from the eye, by placing the official witnesses to the saint's martyrdom on an elevation in the background.

The work reveals not only Rembrandt's debt to Lastman, in the strong outlines, the preoccupation with detail and the emphatic gestures and intense expressions of the crowded figures, but also his own youthful tendency to overstatement. The assassins are not merely throwing stones at the saint; one of them is about to crush his skull with a rock. It is a dreadful scene, and Rembrandt lets the viewer know precisely how he feels about it. Just above the head of St. Stephen, and below the elbow of the man who lifts the rock with both hands, there appears an anguished face, staring with revulsion at the murderers *(page 27)*. It is Rembrandt's own face, the first of his self-portraits.

Another of Rembrandt's hallmarks—an interest in costume—appears in a second very early work, *The Money Changer* of 1627 *(page 32)*, for which his father may have served as model. The coat with which Rembrandt adorned the figure is perhaps a trifle more opulent than might ordinarily have been found in the wardrobe of a Leiden citizen. He took unusual delight in the ornate, Oriental costumes, sumptuous fabrics, jewels and strange objects brought home by Dutch seafarers. His biographer Baldinucci notes: "He often went to public sales by auction; and here he acquired clothes that were old-fashioned and disused as long as they struck him as bizarre and picturesque, and those, even though at times they were downright dirty, he hung on the walls of his studio among the beautiful curiosities which he also took pleasure in possessing, such as every kind of old and modern arms—arrows, halberds, daggers, sabers, knives and so on—and innumerable quantities of exquisite drawings, engravings and medals, and every other thing which he thought a painter might ever need." During his Leiden years Rembrandt probably lacked money to buy such objects in quantity, but later he pursued this interest so passionately that it may have been one of the factors in his financial ruin. His imagination was stimulated by the mere sight of an outlandish turban, a golden helmet or a rich brocade; with the aid of these he was able to transport himself across space and time without plunging himself in books or journeying farther than the auction room. To be sure, he was not a shallow sentimentalist who could be moved to tears by contemplating a plaster cast of an antique bust of Homer, but often a curious studio prop served him as a departure point for a train of thought that ended in a great painting.

Beyond its hint of Rembrandt's fondness for the picturesque, *The Money Changer* is interesting also for its use of hidden lighting; the man holds a coin up to the light to examine it, throwing the illumination backward and to right and left, while the foreground remains in relative darkness. Rembrandt appropriated this device from the works of a school of Dutch painters centered in the town of Utrecht. These men, among them Hendrick Terbrugghen, Dirck van Baburen and in particular Gerrit van Honthorst, had studied the art of the great Caravaggio in Italy and had brought back their personal variations on the master's original light and shadow effects. The pictures of the Utrecht *Caravaggisti* are frequently illuminated by a hidden light source—a trick Caravaggio seldom used, but which his Dutch followers were happy to exploit. In their paintings, a figure or object in the foreground is darkly silhouetted, screening off a lamp, fire or candle that casts its glow on the rest of the scene. Rembrandt had seen the work of the *Caravaggisti*, and their influence on him in his early years was a strong one.

The concealed light in *The Money Changer* serves no function beyond that of drama. However, Rembrandt quickly saw that it could be put to another use—as a substitute for the outmoded halo around the head of Christ—and some two years later he employed it in the first of his painted versions of *Christ at Emmaus*, in which the risen Saviour appears briefly to His disciples. (This subject was of particular fascination to Rembrandt; he would return to it repeatedly in etchings, drawings and paintings in later years.) In the Leiden painting Christ's figure screens off the light, which appears as a supernatural radiance emanating from His body.

To those who think of Rembrandt as a painter of monumental canvases, the diminutive scale of his Leiden works may be surprising. The first *Christ at Emmaus* is only about 15 by 16 inches. Other early works

Rembrandt made these two portraits of his parents shortly before he left home to live in Amsterdam. His father appears heavy-hearted and oblivious to the outside world in this drawing completed only a few months before his death. By contrast, Rembrandt's etching of his mother makes her seem the picture of self-confidence and contentment. Reportedly a deeply devout and serious woman, she outlived her husband by a decade.

HARMAN. GERRITS.

are scarcely larger than the pages of this book, and sometimes smaller; the *Self-Portrait* shown on page 9, for example, is reproduced in its actual size. So far as is known, only one life-size painting survives from the Leiden period—*Esther's Feast*—and this may be Lievens' work rather than Rembrandt's. In the first few years after Rembrandt set himself up as an independent artist he adhered to a tradition that Pieter Lastman had learned from Adam Elsheimer in Italy, painting with marvelous precision on small wooden panels or copper plates. It was not until Rembrandt was 25 or 26 that he began to produce life-size paintings frequently, and still later that he executed such massive works as the *Night Watch*, which is approximately 12 by 14 feet, and the even larger but now mutilated *Conspiracy of Julius Civilis*.

There is no handy explanation for his decision to keep his early art in small scale; possibly he felt that he was not yet ready for works of more ambitious dimensions, although the skill of a painter scarcely relates to the size of the area he chooses to cover. Whatever the reason, Rembrandt's choice of scale seems to have been especially appropriate in the case of his favorite subjects of the Leiden period: narrative scenes from the Bible.

As Rembrandt grew older his spirituality deepened and he no longer saw the Bible merely as a source for dramatic narrative, but at first he chose subjects that suited his great gifts as a storyteller. He turned readily to such passages as Numbers XXII: 27-28 to illustrate the story of Balaam and his ass in a painting known as *The Angel and the Prophet Balaam*. This colorful, sparkling work, painted when the artist was about 20, was evidently highly regarded by Rembrandt's contemporaries; the art dealer Alphonso Lopez, who served as agent for the French crown in the Netherlands, bought it and placed it in his collection alongside paintings by Raphael and Titian. In the same year, Rembrandt produced another jewel-like panel—12 by 16 inches—showing the confrontation of *Tobit and Anna (page 36)*. The "story" of the painting is very slight. Anna, who supports her blind husband by doing "woman's work," has been given a young goat by her employers. The ultra-righteous Tobit cannot believe that the animal is a gift and accuses his wife of having stolen it. Ordinarily, an artist might find scant stimulation in this trivial misunderstanding, but Rembrandt brings to it the deep sense of humanity that illuminates all of his greatest work. The sightless old man appears to be rocking back and forth in shame and grief, while his wife stares at him with a wonderful mixture of compassion and indignation. Although Rembrandt was not yet 21 when he painted *Tobit and Anna*, he had already achieved a depth of perception that no other artist in the Netherlands could match.

Rembrandt's mother served as the model for Anna; indeed, throughout his life he was to paint those who were closest to him, often dressing them in fantastic costumes from his collection, but always seeing in them reflections of universal emotions. In his view, the common people of Leiden or Amsterdam were essentially no different from the towering figures of the Bible, created by the same God, sharing the same mysterious destiny, feeling the same passion and despair. Rembrandt's biographer Sandrart criticized him for spending too much time among "the lower orders" of society, and maintained by implication that Rembrandt might have been a better artist if he had learned to "keep his station." But it was exactly among the "lower orders" that Rembrandt perceived King David or Christ Himself.

In studying the people of Leiden, Rembrandt was particularly impressed by the aged, in whose faces he saw the glow of spiritual riches stored up in years of experience, endurance and meditation. Various local citizens, now unknown, possibly from the ranks of the farmers and tradesmen with whom his father dealt, were models for a brilliant series of philosophers, saints and apostles that he painted from 1627 to 1631. Although all of these works are in the typically small scale of this period, several appear monumental because of Rembrandt's romantic treatment of the background architecture. The worn, rounded walls of a scholar's cell or the archways in a theologian's retreat do not seem to have been constructed by masons but shaped in the stone by the erosion of wind and water, as in the *St. Anastasius* of 1631. There the lonely, rapt figure occupies less than six inches in a panel only about 23 inches high, but to the observer he exists in a limitless world of space and thought.

It is among his pictures of old men that Rembrandt's highly personal, original use of chiaroscuro—the major stylistic principle of his work—first appears to great effect. Chiaroscuro (an Italian word that means bright and dark) refers to the contrast of light and shadow. Italian artists of the Renaissance developed ways of using chiaroscuro to make figures appear three-dimensional, and later Caravaggio and his Dutch followers achieved a striking sculptural quality with the device. But the areas of light and shade employed by Rembrandt's immediate predecessors were sharply contrasted, almost in checkerboard fashion, with few in-between tones. Their figures did, in fact, appear rounded, but because a sense of space was lacking they might have been statues placed against a wall. Rembrandt, working in the penumbra between bright illumination and darkness, developed a pictorial space that appeared boundless, surrounding his figures on all sides. Space itself became a living medium in which the figures were inextricably embedded. The weaving together of light and shadow created a mysterious twilight, constantly fluctuating, emphasizing voids as well as solids. Among Rembrandt's first successful attempts in the use of this device were *The Money Changer* of 1627 and the *St. Paul in Contemplation* of two or three years later. Both gave promise of far greater paintings to come.

Rembrandt's chiaroscuro served him as a means not merely of suggesting space but of expressing the depths of human character and of religious experience. He used the intangible qualities of the visual world—light, air and shadow—to evoke the mysteries of the mind and spirit. He did not master this effect during his Leiden years, but again the loomings of his genius in this regard can be seen in works of that time.

Originally, Rembrandt used the vivid colors favored by Lastman; but by the late 1620s he turned to more delicate hues, using cool harmonies of light blue and yellow, pale green and olive, with backgrounds often in gray. Already, by this time, his color was indissolubly linked to his chiaroscuro. It was used to transmit light and shadow, not merely to achieve a decorative effect.

Rembrandt's handling of paint itself showed a boldness that quickly set him apart from other Dutch artists. He did not apply his pigments in a consistently orthodox manner but set out to exploit the effects that can be achieved by varying textures and the weight of paint. In his *Self-Portrait* of 1629, the wall behind his head is richly textured in shades of gray, while the accents of light on his collar are laid on with a heavy impasto—almost volcanic eruptions of paint upon the surface of the canvas. To give life to his shaggy mane of hair, he repeatedly scratched into the wet paint with the butt end of his brush. In his *Jeremiah* of 1630, which shows the prophet mourning the destruction of Jerusalem, Rembrandt in places scraped the colors down to the red-yellow ground of his panel as though to suggest the embers of a burned city. Among early chroniclers, Houbraken wrote of gemstones and pearls painted by Rembrandt that were "so thick as if they were chiselled," while Baldinucci conjured up a picture of an artist so engrossed in laying on paint that his clothes were constantly dirty, "since it was his custom, when working, to wipe his brushes on himself."

In etching as in painting Rembrandt worked with an inventiveness not seen before his day. In time 17th Century connoisseurs came to prize his etchings even more than his work in oil, and throughout his career his prints enjoyed a good international market. As late as 1669, the year of his death, when according to myth he was languishing in impoverished obscurity, a Sicilian nobleman bought 189 etchings from him.

Before Rembrandt's time the technique of engraving was more frequently used by printmakers than etching. In the former process, the artist works directly on a metal plate, usually copper; to create his design he laboriously cuts lines into its surface with a thin, diagonally sharpened steel rod called a burin. The excess metal thrown up beside the furrow cut by the burin is carefully scraped away before the plate is inked and prints are pulled from it. The visual effect of an engraving is one of neat, regular lines.

In etching, the plate is covered with a protective coat of resin. The artist then scratches his design through the resin with a needle and immerses the plate in a bath of acid, which "bites" the metal wherever the resin has been removed. The action of the acid produces lines of a slightly irregular, vibrating quality; Rembrandt did not regard this as a drawback, however, but as a challenge.

A copper plate lends itself fairly readily to change and correction. Lines may be removed by pounding and burnishing, and added at will; the etcher simply re-covers his plate with a fresh coat of resin and makes new scratches through it. Rembrandt sometimes took several years to finish a plate to his satisfaction, and he sold prints from the various states of his work. It is not uncommon to find as many as four or five different states of the same etching; sometimes the changes are minor, and sometimes radical. Almost from the start of his career, Dutch collectors were eager to purchase the variations. Houbraken, who seems to have been poking fun at the foolishness of some of these buyers, noted that the demand was "so great that people were not considered as true amateurs who did not possess the *Juno* with and without the crown, the *Joseph* with the light and the dark head and so on. Indeed, every one wanted to have *The Woman by the Stove*—for that matter one of his least important etchings—both with and without the stove-key."

In engraving or etching the image is of course reversed—right, on the plate, becomes left on the sheet printed from it. Most printmakers take this into consideration by reversing their designs at the point when they transfer their preparatory drawings to their plates. Rembrandt, however, seems not to have cared much about this; his concern was with the quality rather than the pedantic accuracy of his work. Thus some of his etched self-portraits show him working with what seems to be his left hand although he was in fact right-handed, and some of his signatures appear in backward mirrorscript.

He was so superb an etcher that critics were persuaded that he had discovered a secret process. "He had also a method all his own of gradually treating and finishing his etched plates," wrote Houbraken, "a method which he did not communicate to his pupils. . . . Thus the invention . . . has been buried with the inventor." Indeed, etching has always been regarded as a somewhat mysterious proceeding, and there are "secrets" involving the ingredients in the protective coat, the strength of the acid bath and the time allowed for the acid to bite into the plate. Occasionally the physical or mental health of etchers has been impaired by excessive inhalation of acid fumes, and this, too, contributes to the aura of strangeness and mystery. But Rembrandt had no secret beyond his genius. He was the greatest etcher in the history of art, matched only by van Dyck in certain of his portrait etchings, by Whistler and by Degas in his rare ventures in the field.

Rembrandt's earliest etchings may be dated around 1626, when he was 20, and the very few surviving impressions of such a work as *The*

Cette figure vous montre Comme on Imprime les planches de taille douce.

The process by which engravings and etchings were printed was itself the subject of this print made in the 1640s by a French artist, Abraham Bosse. The worker at the rear dabs ink on a metal plate bearing the design. The man at his side wipes off all of the ink except that in the design's grooves. As the man at right turns the handles of a press, a sheet of damp paper is pressed against the metal plate to pick up an inked impression. Finally, the finished prints are strung on a "clothesline" to dry. Rembrandt may have tackled the entire process singlehandedly, using a press similar to the one shown here to pull proofs of his etchings.

Rest on the Flight to Egypt exhibit both his inexperience and his lively response to the medium. He had no thought of making his print look like an engraving, but used a free, scribbling stroke; the protective covering on his plates was soft, permitting him to move his needle with the fluidity of chalk or pen on paper. *The Rest* is unfinished and experimental, and to many eyes it appears to be a botched job that the artist might better have destroyed. However, the etching serves notice of what is soon to come. As in almost all his work, Rembrandt approached his subject with great warmth, conceiving the Holy Family not in the traditional way but quite literally as a family: Mary feeds her Son while Joseph, who is often relegated to the background in such scenes, holds the dish.

Rembrandt's sense of humanity is even more evident in a group of small etchings of beggars and outcasts made in the late 1620s. In these he was considerably influenced in subject matter and even in pose by the works of the great contemporary French etcher, Jacques Callot. Having seen at first hand the horrors resulting from the Thirty Years' War, Callot produced a gallery of maimed wretches such as might have been found on any highway in Europe. The prints were widely circulated, and there can be little doubt that Rembrandt was familiar with them. Powerful as Callot's prints may be, however, they still contain a faintly satirical quality, as though the artist were asking the viewer, in a detached Gallic manner, "Are they not interesting?" Rembrandt's beggars and cripples are not "interesting," but full of suffering. They arouse a feeling of wrath at the plight of man, and it is plain that he identified himself with them: on an etched sheet of studies of about 1630 there appear the heads of an old man and woman, an aged beggar couple hobbling on sticks, and Rembrandt's face.

Within two or three years after his first efforts Rembrandt had become a master of etching. The portrait of his mother, dated 1628, is an extraordinarily penetrating character study, executed by the 22-year-old artist in a network of very fine lines that capture the play of light, shadow and air with a skill far exceeding that of Callot or of any Dutch etcher. The refinement of his technique appears to even greater advantage in a later portrait of his mother, in 1631, in which countless scurrying, hair-thin strokes are used to build up his chiaroscuro and texture. However—as in the total of Rembrandt's production during his Leiden years—delicacy appears side by side with boldness, even coarseness. In his oils of the period, the contrast may be seen by comparing the precision and polish of *Tobit and Anna* with the 1629 *Self-Portrait,* scored with the handle of the brush. In his etching, Rembrandt's muscular style is vividly apparent in another self-portrait of the same year, in which he experimented with the use of a blunt instrument, probably a broken or double-pointed one, exposing the copper beneath the coating with vigorous slashes like those in a spontaneous pen drawing. The twin currents of refinement and dash, of the smooth and the rough, emerge in Rembrandt's work from the very beginning and are by no means contradictory. They indicate instead the tremendous range of a young man who was able to accomplish more in a few years than many another artist achieves in a lifetime.

Rembrandt's smallest print, shown here in its actual size, reveals his early interest in the exotic dress of the foreigners who frequented Amsterdam when he lived there. He produced this minuscule work, *The Little Polander,* when he was 25 and trying to master the technique of etching; he soon applied what he had learned to larger and vastly more complex compositions.

In the course of his career Rembrandt made scores, even hundreds of impressions from many of his approximately 290 plates. None of the etchings is larger than 21 by 18 inches; many are of postcard size or smaller, and one, *The Little Polander*, measures only three-quarters of an inch wide and two and one-quarter inches high. Rembrandt's income from the sale of his prints is impossible to determine, although the celebrated "Hundred Guilder Print" apparently was so called because an early collector was willing to pay that sum for an impression of it. Today, when a particularly fine impression of a rare Rembrandt etching changes hands, the price may be as high as $84,000, and in the present buoyant state of the art market it will doubtless go higher.

At least 79 of Rembrandt's original plates are still in existence. All are of thin metal, the thickest being only about one twenty-fifth of an inch, and many of them are worn or have been ruined by the reworking of later hands. Astonishingly, no fewer than 75 of the plates are owned by one man, Robert Lee Humber of Greenville, North Carolina, a retired international lawyer, who acquired them in 1938 in Paris but did not place them on exhibition for almost 20 years, during which time the question of their whereabouts continued to mystify Rembrandt scholars. In 1956 Mr. Humber permitted his treasure to be exhibited at the North Carolina Museum of Art, at once settling all the scholarly bafflement. The plates are genuine, and, as recent photographs show *(page 181)*, a few are still in fine condition.

Rembrandt's disdain for tradition in his etching also manifested itself in the third category of his art—drawing. Earlier artists had as a rule regarded drawing primarily as an indispensable preliminary step in the making of a painting or print. Rembrandt made only a few such preparatory studies. The majority of his drawings are self-contained works of art with an independent life of their own. Ordinarily, he made them very rapidly, almost journalistically, with the intention of capturing an idea or impression with a minimum of lines. He seldom disposed of them, just as a writer does not dispose of the notebooks that contain his fleeting ideas, although evidently he could have sold them had he wished. Not long after Rembrandt's death, a French critic and connoisseur, Roger de Piles, noted that he considered Rembrandt's drawings superior to the etchings. Rembrandt was a compulsive draftsman; so many subjects engaged his mind and eye that he must have been involved in drawing almost daily. The 1,400 surviving sketches probably represent only a fraction of his total output.

That Rembrandt as a draftsman worked primarily to please himself may be seen in the great range of subjects that seldom appear elsewhere in his work: women and children in homely domestic scenes, animals, birds, vignettes of random activity in the streets, views of towns and landscapes. These he carefully preserved between blank pages in bound books (24 of which were listed among his possessions at the time of his declaration of insolvency in 1656). Another indication that Rembrandt's drawings were for his own use is the fact that he almost never signed or dated them; as a result, when there was a revival of interest in them in the 19th Century, art historians were hard put to arrange them in chronological order, although today the known evolution of Rembrandt's style makes possible fair judgments about their dates. Among the perhaps 60 drawings that can almost certainly be placed in his Leiden years there are chalk studies of beggars, more summary in style but fully as powerful as his etchings. At least three self-portraits, drawings of his father and mother, and another known as *The Reading*, must also have been produced during this period. Later, he became expert with both the quill and the reed pen, which he often used in conjunction with a wash of warm brown color. Some of his most breathtaking drawings, such as *A Woman Sleeping (page 55)*, were made with a brush alone.

Rembrandt had several pupils in Leiden of whom only one, Gerrit Dou, is of particular consequence. Dou became apprenticed to the master early in 1628, when he was not yet 15 and Rembrandt only 21, and he rapidly assimilated the highly finished style of Rembrandt's small, early paintings. However, while his master later went on to become a giant, Dou was content with a dwarfish if elegant stature. The polished, enamel-like surfaces of his paintings and his almost microscopic detail were very popular in Leiden, and ultimately he became one of the best-paid artists in all of the Netherlands, making a fortune by elaborating on only one facet of Rembrandt's genius. His vogue, in fact, was so great that his paintings consistently brought higher prices than Rembrandt's. Dou made little effort to compete with Rembrandt's use of chiaroscuro for dramatic effects, concentrating instead on details that seem more in the province of a jeweler than a painter. At one point, when he was complimented on his skill in painting a broom no larger than a fingernail, he remarked that the broom was unfinished—he still had three days' work to do on it. Dou's success is typical of that of numerous other Rembrandt pupils in later years; it is doubtful that any of them really understood the great man, but several of them managed to grasp a fraction of him and to make a very good thing of it.

It was inevitable that Rembrandt should sooner or later have departed from Leiden, which despite its University was still a provincial town. The great opportunities were to be found in the rich, cosmopolitan city of Amsterdam. One of the factors that precipitated Rembrandt's move was undoubtedly a visit made to Leiden around 1629 by one of the most remarkable Dutchmen of the 17th Century, Constantin Huygens, who had personal contact with Rembrandt and Jan Lievens and left an account of them in his autobiography.

Constantin Huygens—it is impossible not to salute the man across the centuries—was an exceptionally well-informed connoisseur of art, a statesman, who spent much of his life in the service of the princes of Orange, and the founder of a most distinguished family. His son, Christian, was the astronomer and mathematician who, among other scientific achievements, perfected the pendulum clock and discovered the true nature of the rings of Saturn. Huygens composed his autobiography in Latin, corresponded in French with the writers Corneille and Guez de Balzac and in three languages with the philosopher Descartes, and translated John Donne from English into Dutch (he was a good poet in his own right). Moreover, he was a student of nature, took a most commendable interest in women and was said to be able to mount his horse merely by leaping onto its back. He also had the courage to climb —on the outside—the dizzying spire of the Cathedral of Strasbourg. In the field of painting, he was an accomplished amateur; he might, indeed, have become a professional, but his father did not approve, and he had had to paint in secret. Huygens knew whereof he wrote on the subject of art, having traveled in Italy and England and also having studied at first hand the works of almost every Netherlandish artist worthy of note. Consequently, when he observed that Rembrandt and Lievens—at 24 and 23 respectively—were already peers of the most famous painters and would soon surpass them, his word carried weight.

Huygens found both Lievens and Rembrandt to be tireless workers; in fact, he expressed concern about their health. In this, perhaps, may be found some refutation of the idea that Rembrandt had only to daub his panel to produce a great work; he labored long and hard. Huygens suggested to Rembrandt and Lievens that they make the customary journey to Italy to perfect their art, mentioning Raphael and Michelangelo as the best of exemplars, but the young men were unwilling to go; they were too busy to interrupt their work. Moreover, they said, the finest Italian paintings could be seen close at hand in the Netherlands. This was not accurate: the quantity and quality of Italian art in Dutch hands at the time was not very impressive. But particularly in the case of Rembrandt, the lack of interest in a trip to Italy is significant. He was not then concerned with classical models; the anatomically improbable perfection of Michelangelo's figures may even have amused him. He saw the human body as it actually is, not as the classicists would have it, and in order to find his models it was not necessary to travel to Rome but merely to keep his eyes open as he walked down the street. Rembrandt had no special "pictorial" sense that demanded the superhuman. The human was quite enough.

Rembrandt's desire to stay home did not shock Huygens. He believed, with the traditionalists, that history painting was the highest form of art, but he had a supple mind and did not feel that a classical style was necessary. Indeed, he gave the highest praise to a notably unclassical work of Rembrandt's, the *Judas Returning the Thirty Pieces of Silver* of 1629. To modern tastes there are many other of Rembrandt's paintings that have much stronger appeal, but to Huygens the *Judas* compared favorably with any painting, Italian or Dutch; he found it particularly outstanding in its depiction of the emotion of Judas, his clothes torn, his eye frantic, his hands clasped in supplication for the pardon that he knows it is impossible to obtain.

The enthusiastic endorsement of so eminent a man as Huygens cannot have failed to turn Rembrandt's eyes toward Amsterdam. Moreover, Huygens was not an ineffectual dilettante who contented himself merely with words of praise. In his capacity as an aide to the Prince of Orange, he soon arranged valuable commissions for the artist, who late in 1631 or early in 1632 moved to Holland's greatest city to find almost immediate fame and wealth.

The statesman Constantin Huygens, Rembrandt's first influential admirer, is the dignified subject of this portrait by Thomas de Keyser. Shown with an attendant, Huygens sits before a desk strewn with objects symbolizing the range of his interests, including a *chittarrone* (a kind of lute) and globes of the earth and heavens. Curiously, there are no symbolic references to another of his favorite subjects: painting. Through his key position as private secretary to Prince Frederick Henry of Orange, Huygens was a leading arbiter of Dutch taste, and he used his station to bring young artists like Rembrandt before the public eye.

The Master's Drawings

Rembrandt was one of the greatest draftsmen in the history of art. Because he usually regarded his drawings the way a novelist regards the ideas he jots down in his journal—as a purely private record of observations and feelings—they are often deceptively simple. Yet the very spontaneity and economy with which Rembrandt sketched his impressions make them dazzling to connoisseurs.

His production of drawings was as prolific as it was brilliant. About 1,400 attributed to him survive, and probably at least an equal number have been lost. The reasons for the loss, aside from fire, flood and negligence, may be divined from the drawings that remain. Rembrandt made relatively few preparatory studies for his paintings and even fewer highly finished "presentation" drawings —gifts for friends and admirers. Usually his drawings were unrelated to his major works and were, moreover, unsigned; only about 25 that bear his signature are known. Thus it is likely that inexperienced collectors, misled by the simplicity of the drawings and ignorant of their authorship, discarded them.

Experts estimate the dates of Rembrandt's drawings by studying his style and the way he used his favorite media: red and black chalk, ink and quill or reed pen, brush and washes. All of the drawings on the following pages, unless otherwise specified, are in actual size, and in their range and quality they reveal the warm humanity of a man who deeply loved all life.

Studies of Heads and Figures, c. 1636 (smaller than actual size)

49

Life Study of a Youth Pulling at a Rope, c. 1656–1658 (smaller than actual size)

RIJKSPRENTENKABINET, AMSTERDAM

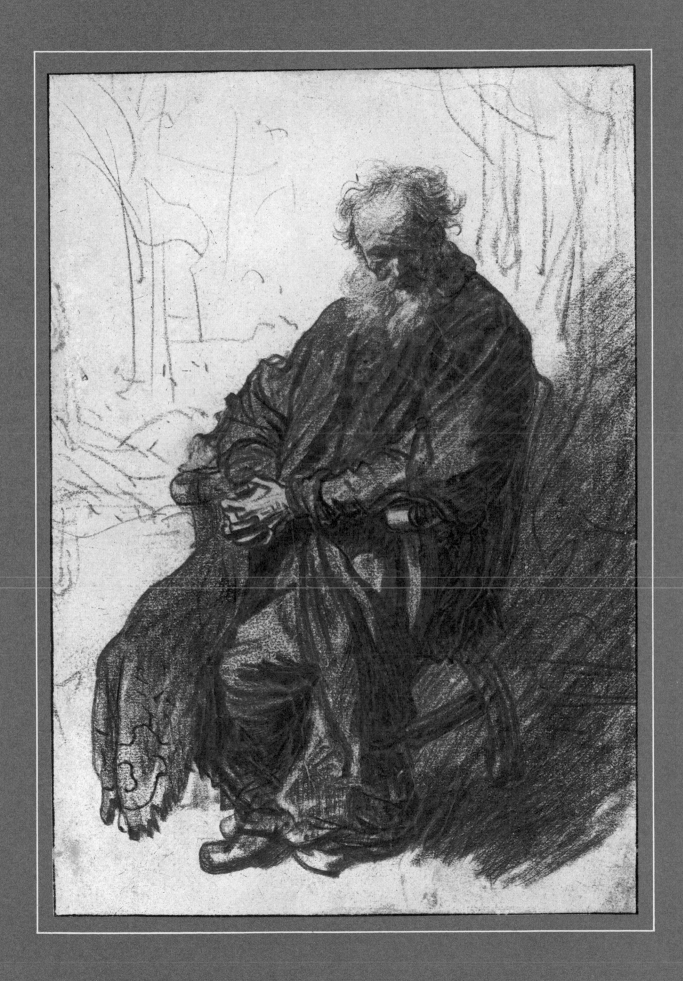

Old Man Seated in an Armchair, c. 1633

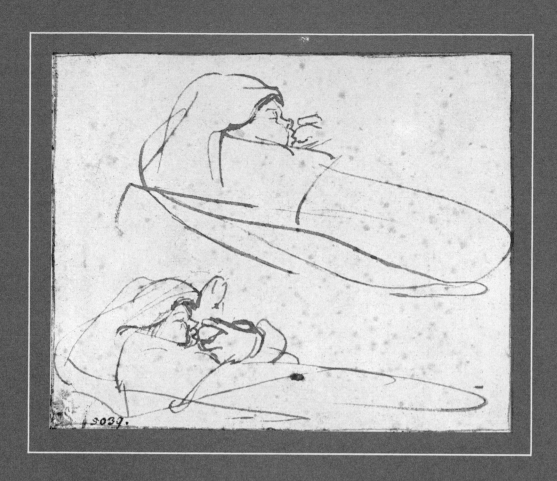

Two Studies of a Baby with a Bottle, c. 1635

STAATLICHE GRAPHISCHE SAMMLUNG, MUNICH

52   *Two Women Teaching a Child to Walk,* c. 1640

THE BRITISH MUSEUM, LONDON

Woman Carrying a Child Downstairs, c. 1636   53

Young Woman at Her Toilet, c. 1632-1635

A Woman Sleeping, c. 1655 (smaller than actual size)   55

An Elephant, in the Background a Group of Spectators, c. 1637 (smaller than actual size)

THE BRITISH MUSEUM, LONDON

Lion Resting, c. 1650-1652

MUSÉE DU LOUVRE, PARIS

57

A Man Seated at a Table Covered with Books, c. 1636-1638

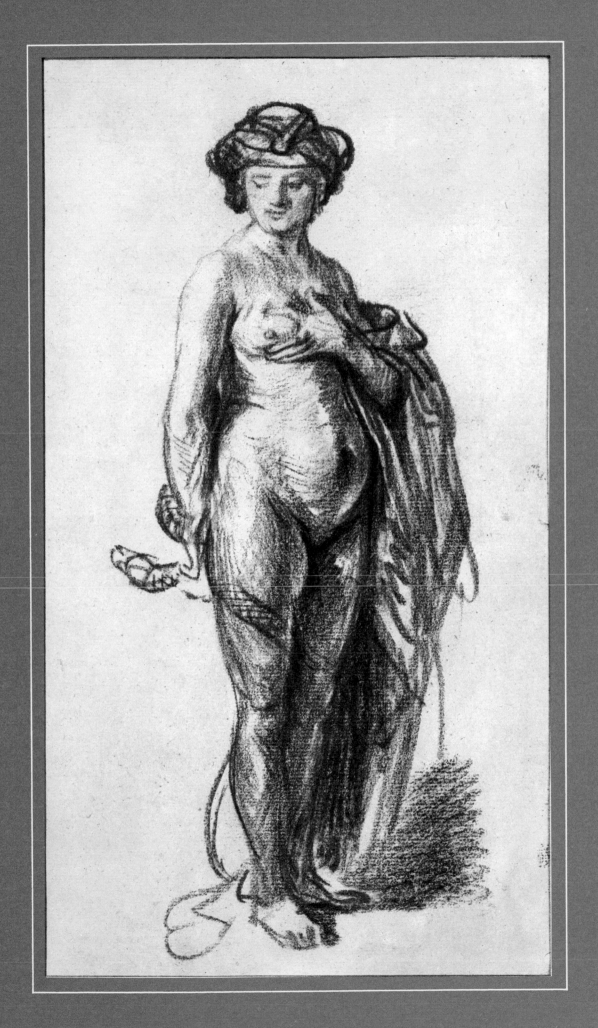

Female Nude with a Snake (probably Cleopatra), c. 1637   59

VILLIERS DAVID, LONDON

III

Prodigal
Years

At the time of Rembrandt's move to Amsterdam in 1631 or 1632 the city was the leading seaport of northern Europe. Merchants and seamen of a dozen nations swarmed along its wharves, creating such a polyglot tumult that one observer noted: "It appears at first not to be the city of any particular people but to be common to all." Crates, bales and barrels overflowed the warehouses; craftsmen plied their trades outside their front doors; wagons and sledges groaned through the streets, and above the rumbling, hammering and shouting could be heard the sound of innumerable church bells sprinkling sanctity on the sharp dealers below. The city was not without cultural interests—it had a fledgling university and a theater—but commerce was its preoccupation. The visiting French philosopher Descartes wrote that "everyone is so engrossed in furthering his own interests that I could spend the whole of my life there without being noticed by a soul."

In its general plan Amsterdam was fan-shaped, with the harbor, stock exchange and town hall at the base and three large semicircular canals, connected by smaller ones, forming the framework. Many of its bridges were arched high enough above water level to permit small-masted boats to pass. Some were so steep that it required immense exertion to move a sledge over them; on the ascent, teamsters eased the way by throwing fat-soaked rags beneath the runners and on the way down spread straw to provide a brake. The bridges were of stone; the same material, and brick, were used for most fine houses, churches and public buildings. Because the city, like Venice, was constructed above a huge swamp, Dutchmen of Rembrandt's time had reservations about the choice of such weighty material and expressed them in a popular verse:

> *The great town of Amsterdam*
> *is built on piles, until*
> *the day the whole place tumbles down:*
> *then who will pay the bill?*

The verse was correct in part: every large building in the city was in fact supported by long, heavy beams formed into trestles and driven through

Rembrandt made this lovely silverpoint of Saskia when he was in the happiest of moods— explained by his words beneath it: "This is drawn after my wife, when she was 21 years old, the third day after our betrothal—the 8th June, 1633."

Saskia, 1633

the estuarial mud into solid ground. But today many 17th Century structures of enormous weight still stand firmly in place, and no one has yet presented a catastrophic bill.

Amsterdam was colorful as well as clamorous. Canal boats, carts, barrels and crates of merchandise were painted red, blue and green. Bright ornamental signs hung from the houses to advertise the trades of the occupants; pastry-cooks used pictures of St. Nicholas, the patron saint of children, while surgeons displayed poles painted in red, white and blue stripes. The red indicated that the surgeon was prepared to bleed his patients, the white that he would pull teeth or set bones, and the blue that he would, if there was nothing more serious to be done, give the customer a shave.

The sights and sounds of Amsterdam were attractive, but Rembrandt was not to be deflected into painting the everyday scenes that appealed so strongly to his countrymen. As a young artist in search of fortune, his chief concern was portraiture, and soon his portraits were in such demand that patrons reportedly had to beseech him to produce them.

Rembrandt's reputation had preceded him from Leiden, and he was regarded, at 25 or 26, as an artist of considerable stature. Soon after his arrival he made a business arrangement with a painter and dealer named Hendrick van Uylenburgh, who operated an "academy," part of which could be more accurately described as an art factory where young men made copies of paintings that van Uylenburgh sold. Rembrandt was already too important an artist to bother with such hack work; however, he lived and worked in van Uylenburgh's house. Precisely what services he performed for his landlord are not known, but his paintings were among those routinely copied by van Uylenburgh's apprentices and exported for sale in the provinces. (In 1637, after the death of the moderately talented artist Lambert Jacobszoon, his effects were found to contain six copies he had made of pictures by Rembrandt. Although not intended to deceive anyone, such "Rembrandts" caused serious problems for later art experts. Today, both in Europe and the United States,

Amsterdam's port, seen in this 17th Century panoramic engraving, mushroomed when the city's shipowners cornered Europe's freight traffic. Ironically, Amsterdam owed much of its prosperity to hostile Spain, which continued its oppressive rule of the city's chief mercantile rival, Antwerp, after the northern Netherlands won independence from the Spanish. Many of Antwerp's Protestants, including experienced merchants, fled to Amsterdam to escape the persecuting zeal of the Spanish Inquisition, and soon helped native residents launch an economic boom that made Amsterdam the hub of Europe's trade.

there are more than a few collectors who believe that they own genuine works by the master, when in fact they own old copies.)

It was probably under van Uylenburgh's roof that Rembrandt painted some of his first commissioned portraits. Although his genius was to seek out and express the inner life of his subjects—this was why, in Leiden, the time-worn faces of the old had fascinated him—in Amsterdam he was obliged to compete in a conventional framework with such accomplished technicians as Thomas de Keyser and Nicolaes Elias. These painters knew very well what the public wanted, and they delivered it: a good likeness, with proper attention to details of dress and ornament, and small attempt to probe beneath the obvious. Young Rembrandt, with financial success still to be won, showed no desire to revise the formula; instead, he met the Amsterdam portraitists on their own ground and surpassed them. His earliest commissioned works, the *Portrait of a Scholar* and *Nicolaes Ruts,* are excellent performances within the accepted limits. They are half-length, with neutral backgrounds and faces and hands in full or almost-full light. Their vitality and strong modeling are far superior to that in the paintings of the fashionable artists, and it is only in comparison with Rembrandt's later work that shortcomings may be seen. Both the scholar and Nicolaes Ruts stare directly at the viewer, seeking to establish a self-conscious communication with him, to let him know that they are substantial Dutch citizens to whom attention must be paid. In the portraiture of his mature years Rembrandt would continue to produce fine likenesses but would add spiritual depths seldom found in his work of the 1630s.

In 1632 Rembrandt painted a group portrait, *The Anatomy Lesson of Dr. Tulp (pages 75-77),* that quickly lifted him to the highest level of public esteem. The group portrait was a long-established and singularly Dutch institution, arising from the desire of the officers of guilds, charitable societies, militia companies and other organizations to decorate the walls of their meetinghouses with memorials to themselves. Customarily a group portrait included at least a half-dozen and sometimes as

CELEBERRIMUM HOLLANDIÆQUE PRIMARIA URBS DELINEATA

AMSTERDAM

het Y

many as 20 or more individuals, each of whom paid a portion of the painter's fee. The commissions were lucrative, but the artistic problem was formidable. Each member of the group, in accord with the sturdy Dutch democratic spirit, expected equal prominence with the others, with the result that the subjects were often arranged in monotonous rows or crescents; a glance at a modern college yearbook, with its photographs of the members of the debating team or the fencing squad, reveals the difficulty.

In *Dr. Tulp,* Rembrandt used a roughly pyramidal composition. The eight men he portrayed—evidently excellent likenesses, to judge from the popularity of the painting—are not arbitrarily arranged; all, with varying degrees of involvement, are witnessing an important event, the dissection of a corpse by Dr. Nicolaas Tulp, a prominent physician of Amsterdam, and there is a unity in the picture that earlier artists had not achieved. The corpse itself, ivory in color, first attracts the eye because it occupies the largest area of light on the canvas, but beside it the dark figure of Dr. Tulp provides a powerful contrast. Save for the crimson of the partially dissected forearm, the other colors in the painting are cool and tend toward monochrome, adding still further to the sense of unity. Another extraordinary feature of the painting is the way the artist achieved balance; by his use of shadow on the right and the prominence he gives to Dr. Tulp, Rembrandt poises seven men against one without in the least throwing his work askew.

The resounding success of *Dr. Tulp* soon brought Rembrandt more commissions for single portraits than he could, or perhaps cared to, handle. At least 65 such works date from the 1630s, and the probability is that several others he produced in that decade have been lost. In another type of portraiture, however—that of double portraits of husbands and wives—Rembrandt's production was very slight. Practical rather than artistic difficulties made such paintings less popular. Dutch houses were narrow and, as a rule, could not conveniently accommodate life-size double portraits. Most husband-and-wife portraits were therefore not attempted on a single large canvas but on two separate smaller ones. In the hands of journeyman artists these proved unimaginative efforts, with little or no psychological relationship established between the two figures. Occasionally, however, an artist of Frans Hals's or Rembrandt's caliber could tie a pair of pictures inextricably together, as Rembrandt did in 1634 in his portraits of Marten Soolmans and his wife Oopjen Coppit. Soolmans stands on the left and gestures as though presenting his wife to someone who has just entered the room, while she lightly plucks at a fold in her skirt, seemingly about to make a slight bow or nod to acknowledge the introduction. Even if these two paintings are separated by a window, door or a piece of furniture, it makes little difference—obviously they belong together.

When there was space in a Dutch house for a large double portrait, the artistic problem was to make the painting a coherent whole and not merely two likenesses that could just as well be cut apart with a knife. The journeyman artist usually did no better with such portraits than with the separate canvases. But in his life-size portrait of *The Shipbuilder and His*

Wife of 1633, which is now one of the adornments of Buckingham Palace, Rembrandt captured his subjects in a moment of interaction that is indivisible—as in the *Tobit and Anna* he had produced in Leiden. The shipbuilder, his caliper barely lifted from the design he is making, is interrupted in his work by his wife, who has suddenly entered the room to deliver a letter; her hand still clasps the door handle. By adding the element of drama to the accuracy of likeness, Rembrandt beautifully solved the double portrait problem, showing a skill far beyond that of any artist of the time save Hals, who was more than 20 years his senior.

Rembrandt's portraiture was financially the most rewarding facet of his art in the 1630s, but it represented only a portion of his output. He continued his Biblical paintings, ventured into mythology, tried his hand (late in the decade) at landscape, and kept on with his non-commissioned portraits of himself and of anonymous people who caught his discerning eye—types known only as *An Old Jew, A Young Officer* or *A Man with a Turban*. Many of his works of the period reflect an unusual joyousness, and for this the reason is not hard to find. While living in van Uylenburgh's house he met the dealer's orphaned cousin, Saskia, the daughter of a wealthy burgomaster of the town of Leeuwarden in the province of Friesland. Evidently he began to court her in 1632, when she was 20 and he 26; he made his first painted portrait of her that year. The young couple became engaged on June 5, 1633, and a few days later Rembrandt made an exquisite drawing of Saskia *(page 60)* in silverpoint, a medium he rarely used, and surely one of the most exacting in all art. Upon a specially prepared surface (in this case white vellum) lines are drawn with a thin silver stylus; there is no possibility of correction—one or two slipped strokes, and the drawing is ruined. Rembrandt made no errors and produced a work that reveals not only his technical skill but his obvious love for the girl.

Rembrandt and Saskia van Uylenburgh were married in 1634. She brought him a large dowry and through her family connections introduced him to levels of Amsterdam society that he might not otherwise have penetrated. The demand for his work increased still further, and into his life and art came an ebullience he never before or later displayed. He indulged his passion for collecting; when he went to auctions, according to Baldinucci, he "bid so high at the outset that no one else came forward to bid; and he said that he did this in order to emphasize the prestige of his profession." In one self-portrait *(page 10),* he pictured himself in the dress of an Oriental potentate, with robes of silk and velvet and a feathered turban, and by casting his light on the right side of his face he somewhat narrowed its "peasant" breadth and achieved a patrician look. His rather theatrical pose, the curving rhythm of the silhouette and the strong chiaroscuro are all in the Baroque style that dominated European art in his century. While the exuberance, movement and melodrama of the so-called High Baroque are absent from this work, it indicates that he had begun to tend in that direction. Soon, when he came briefly under the influence of the flamboyant Flemish master, Peter Paul Rubens, Rembrandt was to plunge into the High Baroque with a vengeance.

In his *Self-Portrait with Saskia (page 11),* in which Rembrandt represents himself as a sword-carrying cavalier in a plumed hat, lifting a great beaker of wine with one hand while he clasps his wife around the waist with the other, both the Baroque style and his own momentary absorption with material comfort are marked. It would be an unfair judgment, however, to place the obvious interpretation on all of this: i.e., Leiden miller's son, having won fame and fortune in the big city, revels in riotous living. In Dutch art the image of a maiden seated on the lap of a laughing man had a well-known meaning: it referred to the Prodigal Son of the Scriptural parable, in gay company before his downfall and his homecoming. Rembrandt was thoroughly familiar with this story and later based one of his most moving paintings on it. Indeed, in 1636, within a year of the *Self-Portrait with Saskia,* the theme of the Prodigal Son first appeared in his etched work. It is by no means inconceivable that in this prosperous decade Rembrandt had some subconscious feeling that he was wandering from his spiritual home and that he would return to it. In the 1640s he did return, both sadder and wiser, to produce a greater art—art that might not have been so lofty if he had not experienced this interlude.

In any case, Rembrandt's religious feeling never deserted him, even in the 1630s; it would deepen constantly until the end of his life. Many works from this decade illustrate the point; it may be well to select one, at the outset, that some early viewers regarded with unalloyed shock (and one that many modern viewers find themselves esthetically unable to cope with). This is an etching of *The Good Samaritan,* dated 1633 *(page 153).* The injured wayfarer is shown being lifted from a horse in front of the inn to which the Samaritan has taken him. A number of human figures, all of them soft-fleshed and lumpish, occupy the center of the composition, and prominent in the right foreground is something worse: an unattractive dog squatting to perform a natural function.

Rembrandt's point—which seems not to have been recognized until Goethe took note of it in an essay almost two centuries later—is that true Christianity is active, not passive. It is all very well for the Samaritan to help the wayfarer; in fact, it is his duty. But if the Creator chose to put into the world people whose bodies fall short of the Greek ideal, man is not to quarrel with this or be revolted by it. Further, if the Creator also saw fit to give life to ugly dogs who are under the same necessity of relieving themselves as a Prince of Orange, man cannot quarrel with that, either. A Christian must have reverence for all life, even if aspects of it occasionally disgust him. This at least seems to have been Rembrandt's understanding of Scripture.

Rembrandt did not find it incongruous, while etching *The Good Samaritan,* to be simultaneously at work on a series of paintings of the Passion for Prince Frederick Henry of Orange—a very important assignment probably obtained for him by his admirer Constantin Huygens. By 1633 he had completed two of the series, an *Elevation* and a *Descent from the Cross.* Later an *Entombment,* a *Resurrection* and an *Ascension* were ordered, and Rembrandt worked on these intermittently until the end of the decade.

Prince Frederick Henry of Orange, the subject of this engraving—actually a copy of a painting by the great Flemish portraitist, Anthony van Dyck—was the titular head of the Dutch Republic during much of Rembrandt's career. Although popular as a military leader, the Prince failed to build a strong government, partly because the Dutch favored decentralization and also because they disapproved of his court. Frederick Henry's intimates spent more time gambling, drinking, fussing over finery and making love than worrying about affairs of state.

In attempting to please the Prince, he faced a difficult problem. Both Frederick Henry and Huygens (despite the latter's regard for Rembrandt) felt that Peter Paul Rubens, then nearing the end of his brilliant career, was the superior artist. Rembrandt must have been aware of this but did not choose to imitate Rubens' style. In the case of one of the commissioned paintings, the *Descent (page 16)*, he did borrow directly from a Rubens work but considerably altered it. He both simplified the composition and boldly moved the central action back into the middle ground, an idea quite foreign to the consummate showmanship of Rubens. Moreover, Rembrandt did not feel constrained, as did Rubens, to make his figures classically dignified or beautiful but painted them with a realism that verged on brutality. Christ, as He is tenderly lowered from the Cross, is a pathetically limp, dead body, without a trace of life that might make His muscles appear "artistically" rendered. There is nothing contrived in the attitudes of the men engaged in their melancholy task; Rembrandt used himself as the model for the one who stands on the ladder holding Christ's arm. In the *Elevation* the artist also appears prominently, as the green-garbed soldier in the center who struggles to erect the dreadfully weighted Cross. If Rembrandt's view of Christianity is recalled, with his capacity for including the dog in *The Good Samaritan*, it is not particularly remarkable that he should have inserted himself into these paintings; indeed, the opposite of vanity is involved here. No other artist has entered so personally and subjectively into the stories of the Bible, and in showing himself helping to raise the Cross, Rembrandt appears to be making a statement frequently heard from the pulpits of today: Christ is still figuratively being crucified, and all men must share the guilt for it.

In connection with the Passion series Rembrandt wrote seven letters to Huygens—all of his correspondence that has been preserved. They are the usual letters from artist to patron, indicating gratitude and discussing money (Rembrandt hoped for more than he got), but they contain one phrase of special interest. In a note of 1639, Rembrandt acknowledges that he has taken a long time to complete two of the paintings, adding that this has been because he has sought to express "die meeste ende die naetuereelste beweechgelickheijt." This can be translated in two ways—either as "the greatest and most innate emotion" or as "the greatest and most natural movement." The difference between "innate emotion" and "natural movement" has occasioned a prolonged and sometimes heated debate among scholars. Many thousands of words have been written in learned journals by students who have felt very strongly in the matter; it does, after all, concern the artist's intent, and it remains the only known phrase in which he ever mentioned it. A convenient means of avoiding the controversy, and possibly the most satisfactory one, is to assume that both interpretations of the throat-clogging word "beweechgelickheijt" may be valid. In the *Entombment*, emotion is the overwhelming force; in the *Resurrection* it is action, or as one critic has put it, the painting is a "turbulent composition with frenzied baroque movement."

One of Rembrandt's letters to Huygens expressed the wish to make him a gift of another painting "10 feet long and 8 feet high" as a token of appreciation. Huygens' reply does not survive, but he seems to have been reluctant to accept this offering. Rembrandt sent it anyway, and from the dimensions, as well as from what is known of Huygens' taste for such subjects, there is good reason to assume that the painting was *The Blinding of Samson (pages 34-35)*. The story of Samson was a Baroque favorite because of its violence and sensuality, and in the Netherlands of the 1630s it had an added attraction: the Dutch had fresh memories of their struggle with Spain, and Samson, the champion of the Jews against Philistine oppression, was an admired figure.

In *The Blinding*, by far the most gruesome of his works, Rembrandt carried the High Baroque as far as he was inclined to go. He never completely abandoned the Baroque style, but after this painting he slowly became more restrained, with his emphasis falling increasingly on "emotion" rather than "movement." It is very likely that *The Blinding* was a special case; in attempting to please Huygens, Rembrandt must have borne in mind his sponsor's taste for the appalling. One of Huygens' favorite paintings was a head of Medusa by Rubens, said to be so terrifying that it was usually kept covered by a curtain. In any case, *The Blinding* boils with horrific action, made all the more dramatic by Rembrandt's clash of light and shadow: Delilah, having cut off Samson's hair, scurries in triumph toward the brilliantly illuminated opening of the tent while Philistine warriors, their armor gleaming in half-light, overwhelm him. One of them plunges a dagger into Samson's eye, and the blood gushes forth while he writhes in monstrous pain. The painting speaks for itself far more forcefully than words can do. It is not a Rembrandt that may hang anywhere but in a museum; a private owner would cover it, too, with a curtain lest he be forced to look at it every day. For all that, it is no mere melodramatic piece of Grand Guignol. Rembrandt's pictorial powers and his psychological insight—as in the face of Delilah—are altogether apparent. If he wished to make plain that he could handle the highest of High Baroque style, he surely did so.

Of Rembrandt's mythological paintings of the 1630s—he did not paint many then or, for that matter, during his entire career—incomparably the most beautiful is the *Danaë* of 1636. (It is now in the Hermitage in Leningrad, which contains one of the greatest collections of Rembrandts in the world, almost all of them amassed by the Empress Catherine the Great in the late 18th Century.) Although the meaning of the *Danaë* has been much discussed, it almost certainly refers to the fable of the Greek king Akrisios, who was warned by an oracle that his daughter, Danaë, would give birth to a son who would kill him. Thus he attempted to keep her in a state of permanent chastity; in the painting *(pages 118-119)*, the weeping cupid at upper right, his hands fettered, is symbolic of this. However, the god Zeus, transforming himself into a shower of golden rain, found his way to Danaë and in time the prophecy was fulfilled.

The nude figure of Danaë—for which Saskia may well have been the model—is the loveliest Rembrandt ever painted and sexually the most explicit; however, it is saved from excessive sensuousness or vulgarity

This unique glimpse of Rembrandt conducting a class in life drawing was sketched during the 1650s by one of his students. He seems to be criticizing one pupil's work as another peers over his shoulder. Others continue sketching the nude who poses on a small dais.

Although students sought him out from the start to the close of his career, Rembrandt was so overpowering as a teacher that most of them stayed with him only briefly before striking out on their own.

by its artistic strength. In his composition Rembrandt substituted for the shower of golden rain a celestial light that enters from the left and washes over the girl. The style of the work is again High Baroque.

The key to the *Danaë* is the girl's upraised hand, which both welcomes her arriving lover and separates the planes between her own figure and the background. Rembrandt was always much concerned with the establishment of depth, and in this instance he succeeded with an ease that can only dishearten other men. Moreover, his modeling, his color, his insight—all the ingredients of a masterwork—are breathtaking. Contemplating the *Danaë*, it is easy to sympathize with a remark made by the German Impressionist Max Liebermann. "Whenever I see a Frans Hals," he said, "I feel the desire to paint; but when I see a Rembrandt, I want to give it up."

Like his mythological works, Rembrandt's landscape paintings are not numerous, and most of them treat quite different aspects of nature from his landscape etchings, which began to appear in quantity only in the 1640s. The etchings are realistic, but when Rembrandt wished to express the romantic he chose to work in oil. A single painted scene—the *Stormy Landscape* of 1638 *(pages 102-103)*—sums up the nature of his work in this field during his first years in Amsterdam. It bears utterly no relation to the flat, orderly, wind-washed Dutch countryside; instead, it contains mountains and a shadowed viaduct lying beneath a mottled, menacing sky. Overwhelmed, almost lost in the foreground, are two tiny human figures that, for all their insignificance in the painting, reveal Rembrandt's eternal preoccupation: even when his subject was the dynamic forces of nature, he could not leave out mankind. (This holds true, as well, in his rare still lifes; human figures appear in all of them.)

Rembrandt's production during the 1630s was so vast that only its surface can be skimmed here. In his paintings, drawings and etchings he turned repeatedly to Saskia as his model. His early studies of her show a very attractive young lady, by the wholesome standards of the time, and seemingly the epitome of robust Dutch health, but as time passed Rembrandt could only record what was true: she was slowly being worn down by some unknown illness. In 1635 she bore a son, Rumbartus, who lived for only two months. In 1638 Saskia's second baby, Cornelia I, also died in infancy, as did her third, Cornelia II, in 1640. Perhaps during the brief life of Cornelia I, Rembrandt made a touching drawing of Saskia with a baby in her lap. Her face—she was then 26—appears to be that of a woman twice her age, weary and resigned.

However much Saskia's illness may have depressed Rembrandt, his art in general did not become infused with melancholy, and he continued to live in a zestful, extravagant style. In 1639 he purchased—with a heavy mortgage—a handsome town house in the St. Anthoniesbreestraat in the Jewish quarter of Amsterdam. Manifestly he felt that his financial success would continue, and perhaps he wished to demonstrate again—as in his profligate bidding at auctions—his belief that fine artists are not merely craftsmen but fully the equals of rich merchants and important officials. Today the house is a Rembrandt museum. It has been increased in height and there have been changes in the façade, but plainly even in

Rembrandt produced many of his mature works in this fashionable town house in Amsterdam. Purchased by the artist in 1639, when he was 33, it proved to be the scene of personal tragedy: his wife and three of his children died here. The house became a financial burden, and in 1660 Rembrandt was forced to move. A new owner added the upper story and roof, giving it the appearance it still bears. In 1911 the Dutch government made it a Rembrandt museum —preserving it both as a shrine to a revered national artist and as an imposing example of 17th Century Dutch architecture.

1639 it must have been a massive investment and a very imposing sight.

By the late 1630s Rembrandt had many pupils; at least 50 Dutch artists served their apprenticeships with him. Among the foremost of the first Amsterdam decade were Govaert Flinck, Jacob Backer and Ferdinand Bol, all very good men whose paintings still command substantial prices. Rembrandt had so many pupils, indeed, that according to Houbraken, he was obliged to rent a warehouse to accommodate them. They worked in cubicles while the master wandered from one to another to make his corrections and suggestions. Houbraken is not always accurate in his dates, but he records a master-and-pupil tale that may well belong to the late 1630s or to the early 1640s.

Houbraken writes of an incident in the warehouse. In one of the cubicles a young student was sketching a female model, and "since young people, especially if there are many of them together, will sometimes get into mischief, so it happened also here. . . . This aroused the curiosity of the others, who, in order not to be heard, in their socks, one after the other, looked on through a chink in the wall made on purpose. Now it happened, on a warm summer's day, that both the painter and the model stripped so as to be stark naked. The merry jokes and words which passed between the two could easily be retold by the spectators of this comedy. About the same time there arrived Rembrandt to see what his pupils were doing and, as was his custom, to teach one after the other; and so he came to the room where the two naked ones were sitting next to one another."

It can safely be assumed that Rembrandt was a man who was not easily shocked; this may be deduced merely from the titles of some of his etchings, without the necessity of reproducing the prints in this volume—*A Man Making Water* and *The French Bed.* The likeliest supposition is that he was much amused by the incident described by Houbraken, but that he still felt, as a master, the obligation to take some action.

As Houbraken goes on to say, "He watched for a while their pranks through the chink that had been made, until among other words he also heard, 'Now we are exactly as Adam and Eve in Paradise, for we are also naked.' On this he knocked at the door with his mahlstick [a padded stick used by an artist as a support for his hand while painting] and called out, to the terror of both, 'But because you are naked you must get out of Paradise.' Having forced his pupil by threats to open the door, he entered, spoiled the Adam and Eve play, transformed comedy into tragedy, and drove away with blows the pretended Adam with his Eve, so that they were only just able, when running down the stairs, to put on part of their clothes, in order not to arrive naked in the street."

However amused Rembrandt may have been at this affair he was by coincidence engaged, at about the same time, in a profoundly serious treatment of *Adam and Eve* that ranks as one of the finest of all his etchings. The subject is of course among the oldest in Western art, and among the most famous representations of it is the 1504 engraving by the German Renaissance master Albrecht Dürer. A comparison of the two works, side by side, reveals much about Renaissance and Baroque viewpoints and much about Rembrandt as man and artist.

At first glance Dürer's engraving may appear to be merely decorative, failing to come to grips with a story that lies, after all, at the center of the predicament of mankind. A magnificently proportioned Eve accepts the fruit from the inconspicuous serpent with apparently no more thought than a girl accepting an hors d'oeuvre, while an equally magnificently proportioned Adam looks on somewhat mindlessly, extending his arm not in a gesture of protest but to display its musculature. It is true that Dürer's primary intent was to present two classical nudes, perfectly posed, but the engraving contains far more than that. Dürer was a scholar and theoretician as well as a great artist, and in his work may be found all manner of thoughts and symbols that are not apparent to the modern eye. The scholar Erwin Panofsky, in *The Life and Art of Albrecht Dürer*, points out several of them. The relationship between the mouse and cat in the lower foreground parallels that between Adam and Eve. The mountain ash to which Adam clings alludes to the Tree of Life, and the parrot perched on its branch symbolizes benevolence and wisdom. Juxtaposed with these are the forbidden fig tree and the devilish serpent. The animals in the engraving are not chosen at random but relate to a complex philosophical doctrine that connected man's fall with the theory of the four "humors" or "temperaments." The cat denotes choleric cruelty, the elk melancholic gloom, the rabbit sanguine sensuality and the ox phlegmatic sluggishness. Altogether Dürer's approach in his subtle and beautiful work is that of a Renaissance intellectual; the classical proportions of Adam and Eve themselves were actually developed with the aid of compass, ruler and geometry.

Rembrandt, although he admired Dürer (the serpent or dragon in his etching is closely patterned after a creature engraved by Dürer), was not a bookman and had little use for theoretics. There are no symbols in his *Adam and Eve*. His approach is highly emotional, and his figures in their nakedness bear no resemblance to the Apollo Belvedere or the Medici Venus. They are only poor mortals, capable of error and of tears. In their faces may be seen a maelstrom of feelings—doubt and desire, craft and innocence, boldness and fear. The tension between them is frightening: man's fate hangs here suspended, and Rembrandt does not call upon the viewer to think but to cry out in warning and despair.

Albrecht Dürer: *Adam and Eve*, 1504

Rembrandt: *Adam and Eve*, 1638

The Prideful Burghers

The group portrait is uniquely Dutch. Alone among Europeans, the Dutch conceived this special art form, brought it to a peak of excellence in the 17th Century and left it as an enduring monument to their satisfaction with themselves. Often called "corporation portraits," these paintings memorialized members of militia companies and of town councils, officers of guilds, and administrators of almshouses, hospitals and other institutions. Occasionally 30 or 40 life-size figures were included in a single work, resulting in a canvas as colossal as a billboard.

The two masters of the corporation portrait were Frans Hals and Rembrandt. Their approaches to the subject offer a clue to their differences in temperament. Hals painted three of his groups in convivial banquet scenes; Rembrandt's four known group portraits—one was all but destroyed by fire—struck a more sober note. Two of his groups attend an anatomy lesson, another convenes on guild affairs, the fourth falls into step on an Amsterdam street.

Whether seen roistering or intent on business, the people portrayed by Hals and Rembrandt shared an understandable vanity; since each member of a group paid part of the artist's fee, each expected not to be slighted in the finished work. But a sense of pride also motivated them; Dutch burghers had a strong civic spirit and were not ashamed to glorify it.

Rembrandt's gift for preserving individual likenesses within the broader context of the group portrait appears in this close-up of Captain Frans Banning Cocq, the central figure of the civic guard depicted in the *Night Watch (pages 82-85)*.

The Company of Captain Frans Banning Cocq and Lieutenant Willem van Ruytenburch (Night Watch), detail

Thomas de Keyser: *The Anatomy Lesson of Dr. Sebastiaen Egbertsz.*, 16

Dutch painters found an intriguing theme in the anatomy lessons given by the surgeons' guild of Amsterdam. Sometimes they were publicly performed, and on these occasions the corpse of an executed criminal was dissected before a large audience, which paid to attend (part of the proceeds of ticket sales went for a lavish banquet for the surgeons).

The Anatomy Lesson of Dr. Sebastiaen Egbertsz. (left) is by a prominent Amsterdam portraitist, Thomas de

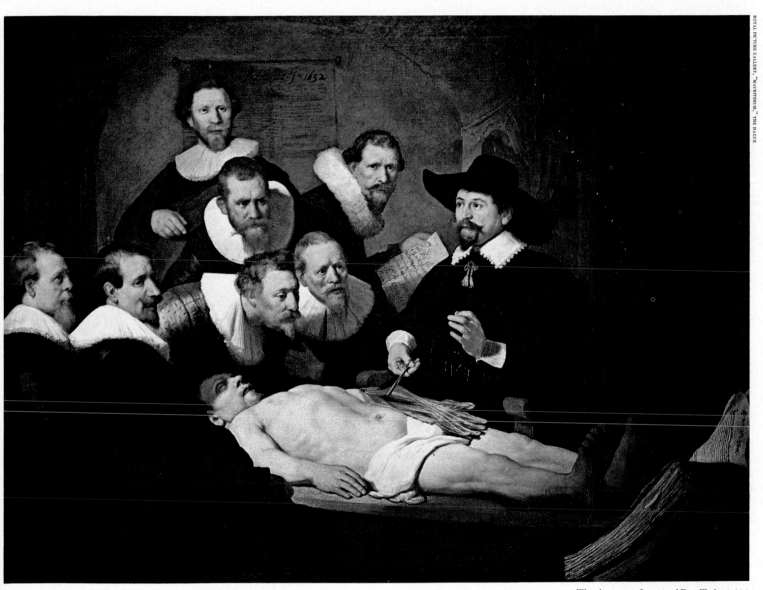

The Anatomy Lesson of Dr. Tulp, 1632

Keyser. For all his proficiency de Keyser produced a static composition. The picture is carefully bisected by the vertical line of the skeleton and balanced by triangles of faces. The effect has little more excitement than might be found in a painting of six men examining a statue rather than the remains of a human being once clothed in flesh and inhabited by dreams.

In Rembrandt's *Anatomy Lesson of Dr. Tulp (right),* all of the observers are involved, in varying degrees, in an affair of deep human significance. The effect is one of drama, not of mere reporting, and the composition is balanced more subtly than de Keyser's. Dr. Tulp (who wears his hat as a mark of his eminent stature) is given such psychological power that he successfully counterpoises seven men. Yet Rembrandt has not violated the canons of good portraiture; as may be seen in the enlarged detail on the following pages, each face is rendered with stunning skill.

Frans Hals ranks with Rembrandt and Jan Vermeer as one of the triumvirs of Dutch art. There is no precedent for the palpitating life he gave his figures or for his spontaneous brushwork. In this portrait of the senior and junior officers of one of the militia companies of the town of Haarlem, a hidden order underlies the lustiness. By

Frans Hals: *Assembly of Officers and Subalterns of the Civic Guards of St. Hadrian at Haarlem,* 1633

varying movement and expression, Hals relates the officers to each other and to the viewer. And, as always, he achieves a rhythmical unity; the positions of the heads suggest the placement of musical notes on a stave, while the upthrust of weapons provides accents that can almost be heard as well as seen.

Frans Hals: *Lady Governors of the Old Men's Home at Haarlem,* c. 1664

Hals lived to a ripe old age; he was more than 80 when he died in 1666. In his final years, he produced this painting of the *Lady Governors of the Old Men's Home at Haarlem,* the charitable institution that, according to erroneous legend, was his last refuge. Another myth holds that the aged artist had lost his touch in this late work. He was, in fact, still in supreme command of his art. As the detail on the opposite page shows, his power of psychological penetration deepened, and there was a gain, not a loss, in his matchless ability to use bold, powerful strokes that simultaneously model form and suggest texture, while creating lively spatial and surface accents. It is a passage that is seldom equaled in Western painting.

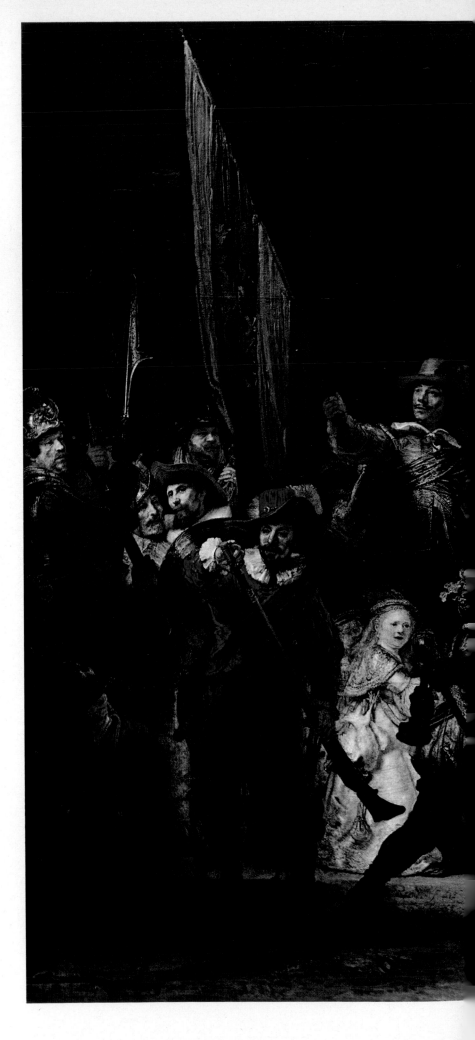

Rembrandt's great *Night Watch* did not meet the usual criteria of group portraiture of his time. Save for the captain and lieutenant in the center foreground, the 18 militiamen who paid for the painting did not receive the prominence they may have hoped for. Instead, they found themselves engulfed in an enormous Baroque work, which is not methodically representational but furiously dramatic—a revolutionary explosion of color and movement. To their credit, the militiamen never recorded an objection to this extraordinary treatment, or to the 16 extraneous figures (who paid nothing) added by Rembrandt to heighten the sense of drama, or even to such unorthodox details as those shown on the following pages. The scurrying little girl —a white bird with bluish-grey feathers at her waist—scarcely merits a proper place among bold soldiers, but she echoes Rembrandt's central accord of red and yellow colors. The mischievous urchin next to her, firing a musket close to the ear of the yellow-clad lieutenant, would also have seemed improper to a lesser artist; actually the flame of the blast blends into the plumes of the officer's hat. While there were no quarrels with Rembrandt's masterpiece during his lifetime, it remained for later pedants to conclude, inexplicably, that the artist had produced a colossal failure, one that precipitated his downfall.

The Company of Captain Frans Banning Cocq and Lieutenant Willem van Ruytenburch (Night Watch), 1642

83

As in *The Anatomy Lesson of Dr. Tulp* 30 years earlier, Rembrandt made the requirements of group portraiture serve his own purposes in *The Syndics of the Drapers' Guild.* Lacking so dramatic a "prop" as a corpse, he sought another means of creating an air of tension and found it by involving the spectator in the picture: the cloth merchants appear momentarily to interrupt their deliberations to focus their attention upon the entering

The Syndics of the Drapers' Guild, 1661

viewer. Soon, it is sensed, they will turn back to their work; but the moment of drama is established.

What is most remarkable in this painting, however, is Rembrandt's probing analysis of his subjects. While he had no reason to flatter businessmen, his natural inclination was to esteem all his fellow men. The result is a shrewd appraisal of men who will acquit themselves with great respect for the guilder, but with honor as well.

IV

Rembrandt's Holland

In 1640 Rembrandt was 34 and, by the standards of his time, was approaching middle age. Both the round-numbered year and the stage of life he was about to enter must have prompted him to take stock of himself, and his *Self-Portrait* of that year *(page 12)* hints at the workings of his mind. There is something searching and faintly quizzical in his look. He has come a long way from Leiden, and now in Amsterdam he is much admired, lives in a great house and mingles with men of authority and wealth, but in his eyes is a suggestion that he has seen enough of mundane success and is becoming disenchanted.

Unlike many artists, Rembrandt was never to become alienated from society; his art will be examined in vain for extremes of bitterness or indignation. Occasionally he produced satirical works, such as his small etching of a monk and a peasant woman fornicating in a field, but this was simply a comment on human behavior rather than an attack on the Catholic Church. He also satirized art criticism in a drawing in which a pundit with donkey's ears discourses pompously on a picture before a gullible crowd while a man in the foreground scatologically expresses his (and Rembrandt's) opinion of the critic. Few artists have failed to make similar comments. In his many studies of tramps, peasants, cripples, beggars and peddlers *(pages 146-147)*, Rembrandt made it clear where his sympathies lay and, by indirection, that he hated oppression and the callousness of economic privilege. Yet there is no evidence that he wished to change his world radically or that he longed to escape it.

Nevertheless, it appears that Rembrandt did not remain comfortable among the rich and socially prominent whose portraits he painted. Their values were not his; he was more at ease with his family and a few friends. The well-to-do Dutchman of the 17th Century, as a rule, thought seriously of only two things—religion and money—but not in the way Rembrandt thought of them. The stern, implacable God of the Calvinists was not credible to him; he never painted a Last Judgment, and he shunned apocalyptic themes. His was the loving, forgiving God of the New Testament. The letter-strict morality of the Calvinists was also foreign to him. He did not ridicule it; he ignored it.

As for money, Rembrandt had a healthy appreciation of it, or rather of what could be done with it. He spent freely on clothing and jewels for his wife and on objects of art and rare curiosities for himself. Among his business-oriented contemporaries, however, the accumulation of money not as a means to an end but for its own sake was the pre-eminent male preoccupation, even exceeding sex—or so foreign observers found. A 17th Century English ambassador to the Dutch Republic, Sir William Temple, noted that "One meets pleasant young gallants, but no mad lovers." When a Dutchman sought diversion from business affairs he was inclined to look for it in drink rather than in women; it was simpler. As a result of this—foreigners thought—Dutchwomen were in a continual state of frustration, and when they were presented with opportunities they took full advantage of them. "To make love like a Dutchwoman" was a common saying in Paris. To be sure, male frigidity was by no means a national affliction, but it does appear that among the bourgeois and upper classes, at least, marriages degenerated fairly early into unimpassioned arrangements. Wives exhausted their energies in frequent and fanatical housecleanings, while husbands pursued the guilder. Again, this was not a situation that could have appealed to Rembrandt. The intimate companionship of a woman was a necessity to him; he could not do without it.

T AMSTERDAM.
By Iacob van Meurs Plaatfnyder en Boeckverkooper inde Nieuwe straet. In de Stadt Meurs, Anno 1663.

Local pride in the wealth of 17th Century Amsterdam found expression in allegories like the one in this engraving—the frontispiece for a history of the city published in 1663. Amsterdam is personified as a queen regally accepting gifts from figures that symbolize four continents: the woman with the parrot represents Asia; the Moor with the camel, Africa; the kneeling queen, Europe; and the Indian with two rolls of tobacco, the Americas. The bearded character at lower right is Neptune, the Roman god of the sea, symbolizing to Amsterdamers the oceans on which their far-flung trading empire depended.

The major fortunes of the Dutch during Rembrandt's time were made in shipping. Fully half of Europe's trade was carried in Dutch freighters, many built in Amsterdam of wood and iron from the Baltic and boasting a capacity of as high as 1,000 tons. More than 2,000 merchant ships in all, a number considerably larger than that under the French or English flags, plied the world's ports. The efficiency of the Dutch and the beggarly wages paid to their captains and crews made it difficult for foreign shipowners to compete.

Dutch merchantmen, moreover, were easily converted into warships. In 1639 Spain, trying to reclaim its authority over the northern Netherlands, sent several score vessels into the English Channel. This armada was met by about two dozen ships under Admiral Maarten Tromp, a Hollander. Although his force was outnumbered, Tromp managed to drive the enemy into the English roadstead near Dover and pin them there. For a month, thousands of Dutch shipwrights worked frantically in the yards along the rivers Scheldt, Maas and Ij, fitting out merchantmen for war, and they were able to increase Tromp's small fleet to 70 combat vessels. With these the Dutch demolished the Spaniards; only 10 of their badly battered ships survived. Tromp, the story goes, then sailed through the Channel with a broom lashed to his masthead in token of his boast that he could sweep the seas clean.

In addition to shipping, another source of Dutch riches stemmed from the far-flung ventures of the East and West India Companies. In effect, the East India Company swung more weight than the weak central government at The Hague; through the pooling of the funds invested by its many stockholders, the Company concentrated the nation's resources of capital and equipment—enabling it to maintain an army of 30,000 men and a fleet of some 50 ships. These heavily armed vessels rounded the

Cape of Good Hope and cruised the Indian Ocean, the Java Sea and the Pacific as far north as Formosa and Japan, establishing fortified outposts in scores of islands and coastal enclaves. The risks were great but the Dutch, conservative and cautious in other matters, were willing to take long chances when large profits might be made. Although thousands of men and countless ships were lost to typhoons, tropical diseases, and rival adventurers from Portugal and England, the East Indiamen brought home fabulous cargoes of rice, indigo and spices. By 1650 the Company's stock certificates were returning 500 per cent a year, and it was with complete justification that the statesman-poet Constantin Huygens could write:

> *How com'st thou, golden swamp, by the abundance of heaven;*
> *Warehouse of East and West, all water and all street,*
> *Two Venices in one, where do thy ramparts end?*

Dutch burghers were so affluent that they thought nothing of ordering specially made porcelain from Canton on the opposite side of the earth, although they often had difficulty in making their orders clear to the Chinese potters. The Dutch preferred floral patterns, coats of arms and Biblical or historical scenes—the plates were sometimes used for wall decorations—and continually admonished the Oriental craftsmen to "paint no dragons or other animals" and "avoid your Chinese fantasies." However, the potters persisted in producing Biblical heroes in Chinese robes and hats, and angels with almond eyes. One wealthy Dutch housewife, wishing to replace a dinner service, sent a chipped cup to China as a pattern and in a few months received her order, fulfilled with absolute fidelity. Every item had an identical nick in it.

In the Americas, the West India Company fared less well than the traders in the East but still extracted fortunes in mahogany and sugar from the coasts of Brazil and Guiana and from the Caribbean islands. Valuable furs—especially beaver and otter—were taken out from New Amsterdam, the capital of a Dutch colony that extended from the Delaware River to the Connecticut and as far inland as Albany. In 1667, two years before Rembrandt's death, the Dutch would be compelled to cede this colony, New Netherlands, to the English—who would rename it New York—in exchange for Surinam, a jungle on the South American coast. The loss of New Netherlands was probably inevitable, but the Dutch might have retained it longer if they had administered it skillfully. Instead, they exploited it with an eye for quick profit, failed to build up a strong colonial population and had small idea of its potential.

There is no record that Rembrandt ever invested a guilder in the West or East India Companies. However, as an artist he was much interested in the objects brought home by seafarers. The inventory of his possessions made in 1656 lists East Indian bowls, a Japanese helmet, Chinese baskets, a "great quantity" of shells and marine specimens, bamboo wind instruments and weapons from the Near East. He also made at least 20 drawings after Indian miniatures of the Mogul school, using subtle, almost Oriental pen strokes and delicate washes on Japanese paper.

The Dutch, like most European maritime nations in Rembrandt's day,

Still thriving today, the manufacture of Dutch tiles was at its peak in Rembrandt's time. Often they depicted such lighthearted subjects as a boy rolling a hoop and a man ice-skating. Found in almost every home in Holland, the tiles served as built-in fireplace decorations and were also made into baseboards to protect the walls during mopping. They were so common in Dutch households that many artists, notably Jan Vermeer and Pieter de Hoogh, frequently included them in their domestic scenes. Rembrandt, interestingly, never used them in his interior settings, subordinating such details to his powerful chiaroscuro effects.

91

Although painting was the art form most popular with the Dutch, a favorite hobby of amateur artists was glass engraving. This 15-inch *roemer,* or wine goblet, was incised by a Rotterdam flax merchant and tax collector. He borrowed his motif—the two irritable gnomes preparing to duel beneath a grape arbor—from a print by the French etcher Jacques Callot, but he executed the work so beautifully that it is now prized as a museum piece. The hobbyist was so proud of the result that he inscribed a couplet below the two figures praising his own achievement, then signed his name and the date of execution: M. van Gelder, 1659.

were heavily engaged in the slave trade. They bought as many as 15,000 Negroes a year at 30 florins a head on the African coast of Angola and sold them in the Americas at 300 to 500 a head. Devout, Bible-reading Dutch captains saw no immorality in the practice and even imagined that God would aid them in adversity. When epidemics broke out among their chained cargoes, they would fire muskets into the air to call the attention of the Deity to the economic losses they were sustaining. Slavery, however, was prohibited in the United Provinces, and if a Negro somehow managed to gain the sanctuary of Dutch soil he was automatically freed. Rembrandt made several pen-and-wash drawings of Negro musicians and mummers, perhaps during a pageant held in 1638 at The Hague to celebrate the marriage of a sister of the Princess of Orange. In these drawings his attention was fixed, as it frequently was, on the colorful and exotic. But his one painting of Negroes, if not an outright indictment of their treatment at European hands, reveals two dignified men who obviously have Rembrandt's respect and sympathy.

At a time when the Netherlands was regarded as the richest nation in Europe, the great prosperity of the upper classes did not descend to the lower. Peasants and urban laborers endured poverty and hardship comparable to that in England a century later at the start of the Industrial Revolution. By 1640 Rembrandt's birthplace of Leiden had 20,000 textile workers, most of whom lived in huts furnished only with straw litter. In a traffic that was little different from the slave trade, children were "recruited" from the highways and orphanages of Flanders and Germany to work in the mills; in one decade, Leiden alone imported 4,000 of them, procured from Liège by one businessman. The Dutch conscience was scarcely pricked by this practice, although in 1646 it was decreed that children should not be forced to work more than 14 hours a day. In Amsterdam, city officials ruled that bakers of fancy cakes must not overdecorate the wares displayed in their windows, "for fear of saddening poor people in whose hearts the sight may arouse covetous instincts."

Despite their penury and their occasional unsuccessful strikes and local rebellions, Dutch workers remained—so foreigners noted—remarkably good-humored. Seemingly unaffected by the puritanical morality of the upper classes, they were sturdy brawlers and drinkers, the sort of men who could be readily understood by Rembrandt, the miller's son who would not "keep his station," and who is said to have remarked, "If I want to give my mind diversion, then it is not honor I seek, but freedom." This is not to imply that the artist was a frequenter of the Holland gin-shops—his biographer Houbraken makes a point of recording that "he spent little at taverns"—or that he did not also seek out the company of intellectuals. Among the latter were a number of Protestant theologians, including Jan Cornelis Sylvius, Cornelis Claesz Anslo and Jan Uytenbogaert, whose portraits he etched or painted. He was on good terms, too, with members of the well-to-do Jewish community who lived near the St. Anthoniesbreestraat where his house stood.

At this time, most of the Jews in the Netherlands—where religious intolerance was leveled primarily at Catholics—were Spanish and Portuguese Jews, or Sephardim, refugees from persecution in the Iberian peninsula. Many, like Rembrandt's friend Menasseh ben Israel, a writer, were men of considerable learning and sensitivity. There were also some north-European Jews, or Ashkenazim, who had fled from countries in that part of the continent and whose cultural level was somewhat lower. Rembrandt appears to have had a wide circle of acquaintances among the Sephardim, including scholars with whom he could discuss the Old Testament in friendly and advanced terms. Through his contacts with Jews—at least 35 of his portraits of them survive, most probably painted for the love of it rather than on commission—Rembrandt became convinced that these men physically resembled the great figures of the Old Testament from whom they were descended, and that idealized Renaissance versions of Jewish heroes were incorrect. This conviction caused him to make some of his rare deviations from Biblical text. David, for example, is described in the Old Testament as fair and handsome; however, in Rembrandt's magnificent painting of David playing his harp to soothe the half-mad King Saul *(pages 174-175)*, the artist used as a model for David a young man—presumably from the Amsterdam Jewish quarter—who was not fair, not handsome, but frail and dark-haired.

So little is known about Rembrandt that not much else can be ventured about his attitude toward Amsterdam society in general except that he had little enthusiasm for a conformist and essentially hypocritical world in which material success was equated with virtue. In his personal habits he seems to have been an abstemious man of fairly simple requirements. The Dutch, although visitors from abroad found them to be execrable cooks, were prodigious eaters. Yet Rembrandt, according to Houbraken, "lived but simply, often content with some bread and cheese or a pickled herring as his whole meal." His round face suggests that he was also plump in body; his full-length self-portrait in Oriental costume *(page 10)* would seem to confirm the notion. However, he may well have chosen to exaggerate his girth in that painting for artistic reasons. In another full-length portrait, a powerfully drawn sketch of himself in studio attire, he also appears to be rotund. But the season in which the drawing was made is unknown; if it was made in winter, Rembrandt was undoubtedly swaddled in layers of clothing to protect himself from the penetrating cold and damp. The British writer Oliver Goldsmith was later to observe that "the true Dutchman cuts the strangest figure in the world. . . . He wears no coat but seven waistcoats and nine pairs of trousers, so that his haunches start somewhere under his armpits." The probability is that Rembrandt was a stocky rather than a fleshy man. The tremendous energy he expended in his work does not coincide with the idea of flabbiness.

As for Rembrandt's personality, at least as it emerges from the scanty evidence to be found outside his art, it appears that he did not suffer fools gladly and that he detested interruptions. Baldinucci reports (at second hand) that he was "different in his mental make-up from other people as regards self-control," and that when he worked "he would not have granted an audience to the first monarch in the world, who would have had to return and return again until he had found him no longer engaged upon the work." Rembrandt could also be abrupt in dealing with

One by-product of the craze for tulips that inexplicably swept the Dutch nation in the 1630s was this resplendent tulip vase. Probably fashioned for a rich burgher, it is a Delftware version of a Chinese pagoda. Each of its 10 compartments, stacked like an elaborate wedding cake, is actually a separate vase holding four blossoms. But so rare, so coveted and so costly were some of the bulbs that a fine house could be purchased for the price of only three exotic specimens, and a king's ransom would have been needed to stock all of the tiers of this vase.

clients. In 1654 he became involved in a dispute with a Portuguese merchant, Diego Andrada, who had ordered a portrait of a young girl and given Rembrandt a 75-guilder deposit for it. When Andrada saw the result, he decided that it was not a proper likeness and asked that the painting be reworked or that his money be returned. Rembrandt told Andrada, in effect, that he did not much care for the opinions of any Portuguese merchant. He would, he said, be willing to submit the work to a committee of his fellow artists of the Guild of St. Luke, and if *they* agreed that it was a poor likeness, he would change it. Furthermore, if Andrada did not like *that* arrangement, Rembrandt would keep the painting and sell it at auction. There is no record of how the matter was settled, but it does appear that even at a time when he was on the verge of bankruptcy, Rembrandt was not in the habit of bowing and scraping.

The dispute with Senhor Andrada provides only a small insight into the artist. Of far greater relevance are the tragedies in Rembrandt's private world that tempered his outlook on life and art during the 1640s. His work became not melancholy but richer, deeper and more restrained, reflecting the mood of a man who has heard "Time's wingèd chariot hurrying near." In the seven years between 1635 and 1642, death struck at his family six times. He lost his three infant children, his mother and his favorite sister-in-law, Titia van Uylenburgh, who had been a frequent visitor in Rembrandt's household; he named his only surviving son Titus, born the year she died, in her honor. Finally, in 1642, came the worst of all calamities, the death of Saskia, a few weeks before her 30th birthday. With extraordinary and painful objectivity Rembrandt made an etching of her during her final illness, rendering her sunken, death-haunted eyes exactly as he saw them. The following year he made a beautiful posthumous portrait of her, as though to obliterate the memory of her suffering and his own, and for this he used the most precious surface he could find, a rare and costly mahogany panel.

This long siege of illnesses and deaths cannot have failed to have had its impact on Rembrandt, although his increasing age and his reaction against the prodigal style of life of his first years in Amsterdam must have affected him as well. Nonetheless, he did not remain depressed. About a year after Saskia's death he was able to produce a drawing called *The Widower,* a delightfully humorous work that shows a man attempting to spoon-feed an infant with the frustration of a plasterer trying to fill a hole in a wall that sometimes clamps shut and at other times moves about. Although some scholars relate *The Widower* directly to Rembrandt's own situation, the drawing is not a self-portrait, and there is no reason to suppose that the infant is Titus. What is significant about the drawing is that it reveals a man with the spiritual strength to resume his work in cruel circumstances.

A few days before her death, Saskia made a will, no doubt with the kindliest of feelings toward her husband, that would later cause him great difficulty. According to the common law, half of their joint estate belonged to Rembrandt, while Saskia was permitted to dispose of her half as she saw fit. She left it to Titus, stipulating that her husband should receive the interest from it until Titus married or came of age. In drawing up the will, she could not have foreseen that Rembrandt's financial success would not continue. Thus, perhaps assuming that her husband would never have trouble providing for their boy, Saskia added a further stipulation: if Rembrandt were to remarry, her half of the estate would go not to Titus but to one of her sisters, and with it would go the interest.

Not long after Saskia's death, Rembrandt was confronted with the problem he made light of in *The Widower*: with no woman in his household, how was he to care for an infant? Accordingly, he hired a nurse named Geertghe Dircx, who was probably of peasant stock, and the widow of a trumpeter. Apparently she had a difficult and even hysterical temperament. Rembrandt made two drawings of a woman generally thought to be Geertghe. In one, she appears heavy-faced, with an abstracted look; in the other, her back is turned to the artist.

Geertghe probably entered Rembrandt's household around 1642; but she became a burden to him, and after seven years he dismissed her. She then brought a lawsuit against him, maintaining that he had promised to marry her and had given her a ring in token of his intent. Rembrandt denied the allegation. In fact, he was in no position to remarry. Had he done so, he would have been obliged, under the terms of Saskia's will, to forfeit the income he was receiving from his young son's inheritance. Although the income was not large, Rembrandt was already in straitened circumstances and needed every guilder he could get. Despite his denial of any promise to Geertghe, the Dutch court was unconvinced, and he was ordered to pay 200 guilders a year for her support. In 1650 she was confined to a house of correction in the town of Gouda; there is good reason to believe that Rembrandt was responsible for her commitment. In any event, this circumstance did not free him from his obligation. He continued to pay for her maintenance until her release in 1655.

This self-portrait of Rembrandt at 42 shows him at his studio window, holding an etching needle. Along with the practical references to his craft—rare in earlier self-characterizations—a new searching analysis of personality appears in this work, the beginning of the series of self-portraits he made during his last decades.

Some time in the mid-1640s Rembrandt had brought into his household a second woman named Hendrickje Stoffels, who first served him as a maid. The daughter of a soldier from Bredevoort, she was 20 years younger than the artist and of a far different temperament from Geertghe. From what may be discerned in Rembrandt's many drawings and paintings of Hendrickje, she was a gentle, simple, warm-hearted soul, ideally suited to be the companion of an increasingly troubled man. Evidently her relationship to Rembrandt very soon changed from that of servant to model to wife in all but name, and she remained with him until her death at 37 in 1663. While still in her early twenties, Hendrickje bore him an illegitimate child, who died in infancy, and two years later she bore another, a daughter, who survived both Rembrandt and herself. (The artist, unshaken by the deaths of Saskia's children Cornelia I and Cornelia II, gave that name to Hendrickje's daughter as well.)

By 1648 Rembrandt had more or less reassessed his world and his art. The etching he made of himself at that time reveals a man who is not melancholy, but who knows misfortune; not grim, but charged with an awesome determination. In his personal life he was sustained by the presence of Hendrickje and of Titus, in whom he took immense delight, and as an artist he was about to enter a new realm of creation that few other men have been privileged to discover.

Landscapes: Real and Romantic

Dutchmen of the 17th Century were extremely fond of landscape pictures. Many thousands of these works, sensitive, simple and full of charm, still survive to delight connoisseurs. So great was the vogue for them in their own time that landscape, itself a specialty, was divided into sub-specialties. Some artists dealt only in scenes of canals and dunes; others concentrated on town panoramas, marine views, woods, winter pictures or moonlit ones.

Rembrandt's involvement with landscape lasted less than 20 years, from his early 30s to his late 40s. His outdoor scenes constitute little more than a tenth of his total production, yet they reveal the same wide-ranging quality that marks his work in other fields. Some of Rembrandt's landscapes are romantic and visionary; others are wholly realistic.

With rare exceptions, he used the medium of oil paint to express his more imaginative concepts of nature. He reserved his realism in landscapes almost entirely for etchings and drawings. Even here, however, he developed a free, "shorthand" style that went beyond mere faithful reproduction. Not only did he reduce the complexities of the visible scene, but, through a process of exquisite selection, he emphasized what was important in that scene, providing the viewer with exactly the material, and none other, that enables him to follow Rembrandt into the artist's world.

This pen and wash drawing combines Rembrandt's early flair for the dramatic with a fresh appreciation of the homely charm of his native countryside. The passing storm is drawn with hasty violence, the cottages and people with deliberate and affectionate precision.

Cottages before a Stormy Sky in Sunlight,

Six's Bridge, 1645

View over the Ij from the Diemerdijk, c. 1650-1653

On Rembrandt's excursions into the open country around Amsterdam he frequently followed the waterways. Above, slightly enlarged, is a drawing of the early 1650s, showing the expanse of the river Ij and the small town of Spaarndam on the far shore. The horizon divides the picture almost exactly in half, an especially effective device for emphasizing the overpowering flatness of the landscape. With his economy of line, Rembrandt has only to note the bending of a few reeds in the foreground to evoke the clean breeze that washes over all. By relying on blank areas of his paper and a few sensitively placed accents, he suggests the lightness of the air, while by leaving untouched the whiteness of the surfaces of a few crude boards, he instantly summons up the idea of sunlight.

The etching at left, slightly reduced from its actual size, is the famous *Six's Bridge,* which Rembrandt purportedly produced in an hour or two while visiting the country estate of his friend Jan Six. Here again the artist's extraordinary economy of means is apparent. These are not particular but generic trees, and the bare rigging of the boat responds not to any one meteorological condition of the day but to the eternal winds that Shakespeare called "viewless."

99

The Windmill, 1641

The Omval, 1645

Winter Scene, 1646

At first glance, these three scenes seem no more than a summing-up of the most typical aspects of the Dutch countryside, still familiar to travelers in Holland today: a windmill, a low-lying village vista, a placid farm in wintertime. Yet each in its own way says something about Rembrandt's complexity as an artist. His etching of *The Windmill (opposite, top)* is no mere representation but a study in personality; the mill becomes a sturdy sentinel standing guard over its owner's fortunes. The etching below it is ostensibly no more than a simple view of a hamlet near Amsterdam called The Omval; but Rembrandt has hidden two lovers in the dark recesses of the willow at left, and in the prominence given the figure on the riverbank he makes a point about the inexorable bond between man and nature.

He reverts to this theme in the *Winter Scene* above, a work that is an exception among his painted landscapes for several reasons. It is one of Rembrandt's rare ventures into landscape realism in a painting; moreover, he made it in tiny dimensions—it is shown actual size—in a period when he was producing canvases fully 50 times as large; and, unlike most of his more ambitious landscapes, it is signed and dated. In the self-confidence of his maturity, Rembrandt seemed to be offering this little work as testimony of his ability to break with his own artistic past whenever he so chose.

101

When Rembrandt wished to take a romantic approach to nature, as he did in most of his landscape paintings, he pulled out all the stops. His *Stormy Landscape* has no real relation to the Dutch scene; instead it features skull-eyed ruins, decaying towers and a general fist-shaking vehemence. In this work Rembrandt was notably influenced by the fantastic panoramic landscapes of his predecessor Hercules Seghers. One admiring Dutch contemporary, trying to explain the broad sweep and imaginative scope of Seghers' vistas, wrote that "it is as if he went pregnant with entire provinces to which he gave birth with enormous expanses, strangely illustrated. . . ." It is a description that sums up Rembrandt's visionary landscapes as well; however, he abandoned this type of painting when he was about 45 and never returned to it.

Stormy Landscape, c. 1638

104

V

An Exploration
of Styles

A favorite Rembrandt theme was the supper at Emmaus, where the resurrected Christ revealed Himself. Early versions stress the excitement of the moment of revelation; this mature work stresses the Saviour's serenity.

Christ at Emmaus, 1648

It is customary and convenient to compartmentalize the lifework of artists—youth, middle, mature, late—but there is also something colossally impertinent about it. This seems particularly true in the case of Rembrandt, whose artistic legacy was so large and who left so few words of self-explanation or defense. The thought of encountering the artist ages hence, in some celestial dark alley, should give pause to anyone who presumes to make pronouncements about him now.

What follows, it should quickly be said, is not an individual judgment but a consensus. Perhaps without exception, students of Rembrandt agree that he did indeed have a "middle" or "transitional" period, and that this occurred approximately between 1640 and 1648, the 34th to the 42nd years of his life. There is also general agreement as to the nature of the transition—the problems he faced and resolved.

Rembrandt was an artist of the Baroque; he was born and died in that tradition. He could no more have escaped the Baroque than any artist can escape the style of his time. Around 1640, however, having explored and employed the Baroque elements of turbulent motion, dramatic diagonals, curving lines and clashing light and shadow, Rembrandt sought other means of expressing the simpler, quieter, more profound feelings within himself. He found the means in classicism, by looking back to the work of the masters of the Renaissance. Throughout the 1640s Rembrandt's Baroque elements and his tendency to the classical ran together in his art, sometimes mingling, sometimes with one assuming ascendancy over the other, until at the end of the decade the classical became predominant. To be sure, Rembrandt never became an outright classicist; he was far too independent of mind, too much a realist, and too much a 17th Century Dutchman for that. But slowly he did come to accept certain classical devices that he found suited to the calmness and wisdom of his maturity.

If one reads the accounts of Rembrandt's early biographers or looks at many of his early pictures, it seems remarkable that he ever accepted *anything* from the classical world. What the German artist Joachim von Sandrart, who knew him in Amsterdam, wrote about him had some truth in it: "[Rembrandt] did not hesitate to oppose and contradict our rules of art—such as anatomy and the proportions of the human body—perspective and the usefulness of classical statues, Raphael's drawing and judicious pictorial disposition, and the academies which are so particularly necessary for our profession." Indeed, from his earliest years Rembrandt had a pronounced vein of anti-classicism that sometimes extended to satire. His etching of a pot-bellied *Nude Seated on a Mound* of about 1631 *(page 152)* reveals a gross human being whose body, seemingly soft as custard, was antithetical to the goddess-types of the Renaissance. Works of this sort were no doubt what the Dutch writer Andries Pels had in mind in a poem published in 1681 in which he referred to Rembrandt thus:

> He chose no Greek Venus as his model,
> But rather a washerwoman or a treader of peat from a barn
> And called this whim "imitation of nature."
> Everything else to him was idle ornament. Flabby breasts,
> Ill-shaped hands, nay, the traces of the lacings
> Of the corsets on the stomach, of the garters on the legs,
> Must be visible, if nature was to get her due.
> This is his nature, which would stand no rules,
> No principles of proportion in the human body.

Rembrandt objected not only to the implausible classical nude, but also to classical pictorial clichés. For example, the myths of antiquity abound in rapes, and classical painters could hardly avoid this subject; in fact they welcomed the opportunity it provided for drama. In conventional rape scenes it was customary for the victims to throw their arms in Y-shape in the air to indicate the dire fate that was overtaking them. To Rembrandt this was incredible: does not a lady put up a struggle? In his own *Rape of Proserpine* of the early 1630s he showed her clutching for Pluto's throat with one hand while she clawed at his cheek with the other. One of Rembrandt's genre drawings of around 1635, *The Screaming Boy,* is a wonderfully animated scene of an annoyed woman struggling with a squalling, kicking brat—and from this drawing the artist drew the inspiration for a mythological painting, *Ganymede Caught Up by the Eagle,* which has often been regarded as one of the most revolting, grotesque works ever to come from his hand. But it is highly likely that the painting is what might today be called a "put-on." Michelangelo, Correggio, Rubens and other painters had been able to treat seriously the myth of Ganymede, the youthful prince who was so handsome that the lecherous god Zeus, in the guise of an eagle, flew off with him to Olympus; Rembrandt could not. Apparently he found something ridiculous in the idea of a muscular young hero about to be sexually assaulted in mid-air by a gigantic bird. Rembrandt's Ganymede is not a Greek hero but the above-mentioned Amsterdam brat, and the entire painting —which only the most forthright of Dutch burghers would have wanted hung permanently in his house—is not dramatic but coarsely funny.

Rembrandt's anti-classicism, however, was by no means all-inclusive: it simply reflected the view of a man who believed what he saw in the world around him and refused to believe what was manifestly silly—at least in the context of 17th Century Holland. After Rembrandt had set aside the elements of classicism that he found ludicrous, there still remained much that he deeply admired. He had a large collection of prints that had been made after the paintings of such Renaissance giants as Titian, Leonardo, Mantegna, Dürer and (Sandrart's statement to the contrary) Raphael. He made both close and free copies of these prints and on several occasions used their motifs in his own work. He also had in his own collection (Sandrart again to the contrary) a number of casts of antique statues and busts, which he employed as models—not in order to echo their unlikely physical perfection, but because of the stimulus they gave to his spirit, as in the *Aristotle Contemplating the Bust of Homer (page 125)*. But primarily what the mature Rembrandt took from the classical world were qualities of breadth, simplicity and solemnity, of the timeless and the true. Or perhaps more accurately, he did not take these qualities but came to share them, as have all great Western artists from the 15th Century to the 20th.

A clear foreshadowing of his turn toward classicism can be seen in Rembrandt's *Self-Portrait* of 1640 *(page 12)*. A year earlier he had seen a portrait of Baldassare Castiglione by Raphael, painted around 1515, which had been offered for sale at an Amsterdam auction. Rembrandt had more than a passing interest in the painting and may even have bid unsuccessfully for it; he made a hasty pen sketch of it and noted in the margin that it brought the high price of 3,500 guilders. Around the same time he must have seen Titian's so-called *Portrait of Ariosto,* which appeared on the lively Amsterdam art market in the late 1630s. He soon translated the classical spirit of Raphael's and Titian's works into his own: his *Self-Portrait* has great calm and balance. The composition of the picture is roughly pyramidal, as Raphael or Titian might have made it, and there are stabilizing horizontal lines typical of the Renaissance: the stone sill on which Rembrandt rests his arm, the arm itself, the lines of his face and even of his hat.

The appearance of classical elements in one painting, however, did not signal that Rembrandt had suddenly taken a new direction in his art and would not retrace his steps. His "transitional" period was a time when he alternated between one mood and another. In his most famous picture, the *Night Watch* of 1642 *(pages 73, 82-85),* only a hint of the classical—in the background architecture—can be seen. The painting is a masterpiece of the Baroque.

Since this celebrated work will always be known by an incorrect title, and since those who have not seen it continue to believe, quite logically, that it is a nocturnal scene, a discussion of its name and its "darkness" seems worthwhile before turning to the painting itself. Its formal title is *The Company of Captain Frans Banning Cocq and Lieutenant Willem van Ruytenburch,* and not until late in the 18th Century did it acquire the name by which it is now known. Unfortunately, both "Night" and "Watch" are wrong. The civic guards who are depicted had, by the time Rembrandt painted them, become quite pacific; it was no longer necessary for them to defend the ramparts of Amsterdam or to go out on

At an art auction in 1639 Rembrandt made this sketch of Baldassare Castiglione, an Italian diplomat and writer, from a portrait by Raphael. The hurried copy reflects Rembrandt's increasing interest in the Italian Renaissance painters, whose work he was occasionally exposed to at the auctions in Amsterdam's busy art market. His scribbling on this sketch indicates that the Raphael was part of the collection of a prominent Amsterdam connoisseur.

watches by night or by day. Their meetings had been diverted chiefly to social or sporting purposes; if they may be said to have any particular destination in the painting, it is perhaps to march into the fields for a shooting contest or to take part in a parade.

"Night" is even less apt than "Watch." When the critics and the public attached that word to the painting, the canvas had become so darkened by dirt and layers of varnish that it was difficult to tell whether the illumination Rembrandt had provided in it came from the sun or moon. Not until after the end of World War II was the painting fully restored so that the viewer could get an idea of the brightness it had when it left Rembrandt's hand more than 300 years before. (Upon seeing the refreshed work, journalists promptly re-christened it the "Day Watch.")

Rembrandt, possibly more than any other artist, has suffered from the ministrations of picture restorers. The infamous "Rembrandt brown" is their work, not his, and so too is the widespread impression that he was a monotonous colorist who invariably worked with a low-keyed palette. It is true that the forceful use of chiaroscuro in his paintings, with its emphasis on the mysterious, evocative qualities of shadow, has always disturbed certain critics, and so occasionally has his subject matter. John Ruskin, the 19th Century English art critic and essayist, who had a superb knack for being wrong in just the right words, remarked that "it is the aim of the best painters to paint the noblest things they can see by sunlight, but of Rembrandt to paint the foulest things he could see by rushlight." However even Ruskin, if he had seen a cleaned Rembrandt panel or canvas, might have directed some of his vitriol at the men who applied layer upon layer of toned varnish on the artist's pictures. In the past generation not only the *Night Watch* but many other Rembrandt paintings have been stripped of their dirty and discolored overlays—with a consequent reappraisal by critics of his genius as a colorist.

There is an understandable, if not a good, reason why Rembrandt's works were so slathered with varnish. As he matured he became increasingly free in his technique, using bold strokes, passages of broken color, heavy impasto applied with the palette knife, and areas scumbled with his fingers. This highly personal style proved a mystery to most critics of the late 17th and 18th Centuries, who attributed it to laxness or perversity. Rembrandt himself seems to have suggested indirectly that his work was to be observed at a slight distance, so that the intervening space would make his strokes and colors fuse. According to Houbraken, "visitors to his studio who wanted to look at his works closely were frightened away by his saying, 'The smell of the colors will bother you.'" The probability is that Rembrandt was not at all concerned about the smell of fresh paint, which is pleasant to many people, but that he did not care to answer dim questions from his guests.

To their credit, it should be recorded that there were a few early critics who admired Rembrandt's rough strokes and said so. In 1700 an English writer on art, John Elsum, published a poem dedicated to "An Old Man's Head, by Rembrant":

> *What a coarse rugged Way of Painting's here,*
> *Stroaks upon Stroaks, Dabbs upon Dabbs appear.*

The Work you'd think was huddled up in haste,
But mark how truly ev'ry Colour's placed,
With such Oeconomy in such a sort,
That they each mutually support.
Rembrant! thy Pencil plays a subtil Part
This Roughness is contriv'd to hide thy Art.

One or two theorists of Rembrandt's era agreed that his paintings, in their "coarse rugged Way," would appear more coherent if one stepped back from them, but they noted that a similar coherence could be obtained with varnish. As a result, for more than a century after Rembrandt's death liberal applications of varnish, frequently tinted, were applied to many of his paintings by dealers and—what is even more unfortunate—by collectors. Theoretically, the *Night Watch* should not have been a candidate for such treatment. Although it contains some wonderfully rich and complex areas, Rembrandt did not paint it in the freest style he would ultimately achieve. Nonetheless, this masterpiece received its full gallonage of Golden Glow and Toner. (How severely Rembrandt's paintings suffered from such applications may be seen in the color plate on page 180, which shows a half-cleaned work.) In fairness to the varnishers, it must be said that their intention was to protect the paintings from dirt as well as to "improve" certain of them by making the strokes and colors blend. Inadvertently, the varnishers also rendered a great service to the world of art. In 1911, when the *Night Watch* was still covered with a thick layer of hardened varnish, an unemployed ship's cook went at it with a knife. He seems to have had no reason for this act of apparent madness beyond the fact that the painting was famous and he was not. But its surface coating proved as resistant as glass, and the attacker was unable to cut through it.

The *Night Watch* was commissioned by Captain Banning Cocq and 17 members of his civic guards; that this was the total of Rembrandt's clients for the work is assumed from the fact that 18 names, added by an unknown hand after the painting was completed, appear on a shield on the background wall. Doubtless the guardsmen expected a group portrait in which each member would be clearly recognizable, although perhaps not of equal prominence; it was often the practice for less affluent or junior members of a group to be represented only by heads or partial figures, for which they paid less than did those who were portrayed full length. The guardsmen, most of whom must have been familiar with Rembrandt's *Anatomy Lesson of Dr. Tulp* of a decade earlier, may also have foreseen that the artist would not produce a standard, static painting. But none of them could have been prepared for the thunderous masterwork with which they were confronted.

The *Night Watch* is colossal. In its original dimensions it measured approximately 13 by 16 feet and contained not only the 18 guardsmen but 16 other figures added by Rembrandt to give still more animation to an already tumultuous scene. It was by far the most revolutionary painting Rembrandt had yet made, transforming the traditional Dutch group portrait into a dazzling blaze of light, color and motion, and subordinating the requirements of orthodox portraiture to a far larger, more complex but still unified whole. In Rembrandt's hands what was, after all, a commonplace affair became filled with Baroque pictorial splendor, loud with the sound of drum and musket, the thud of ramrods, the barking of a dog, the cries of children. In the forefront Captain Banning Cocq—in black, with a red sash—and his lieutenant in yellow lead the forward drive of the still unformed ranks. The sense of movement is reinforced by converging diagonal lines: on the right, the foreshortened spontoon in the lieutenant's hand, the musket above it and the lance still higher; and on the left, the captain's staff, its line repeated above by another musket and the banner. The effect on the viewer is direct; he feels that he had best get out of the way.

The powerful contrast of light and shade heightens the sense of movement, but it is well to regard Rembrandt's use of light in this painting, as in many others, from an esthetic rather than from a strictly logical viewpoint. He was, in the phrase of one critic, "his own sun-god." The shadow cast by the captain's hand on the lieutenant's coat might suggest that the sun is at an apparent angle of about 45 degrees to the left, but the shadow of the captain's extended leg indicates quite a different angle. The picture was of course composed and painted indoors, not while the officers posed for him out of doors, and although his lighting in any particular detail may be true to nature, that is not the case overall. He regulated and manipulated light—opening or closing the shutters in his studio—for his own purpose, which was to create an atmosphere both dreamlike and dramatic.

The *Night Watch* lies at the center of the most persistent and annoying of all Rembrandt myths. As recently as the tourist season of 1967, KLM Royal Dutch Airlines featured the painting by their illustrious countryman in an advertisement inviting travelers to visit Holland. "See *Night Watch*," said the advertisement, "Rembrandt's spectacular 'failure' [that caused him to be] hooted . . . down the road to bankruptcy." The myth has been attacked by various critics, and a few years ago it was utterly demolished by Professor Seymour Slive of Harvard in *Rembrandt and His Critics.* But since the tale has a phoenixlike capacity for self-resurrection, a few of Professor Slive's observations will bear repeating here.

The painting was *not* poorly received; no critic during Rembrandt's lifetime wrote a word in dispraise of it. Captain Banning Cocq himself had a watercolor made of it for his personal album, and a contemporary oil copy of it by Gerrit Lundens, now owned by the National Gallery in London, offers further proof of the picture's popularity. The *Night Watch* was never hidden in some obscure location; it was first hung in the Kloveniersdoelen, the headquarters of the civic guardsmen, and in 1715 it was moved to the Amsterdam town hall, as prominent a place as could have been found for it. (Probably on the occasion of its transferral, and no doubt for reasons of space, the painting was cut down on all four sides. The greatest loss was on the left, where a strip about two feet wide, containing three figures, was removed.) Nor did painting this supposed "failure" result in any abrupt withdrawal of patronage; Rembrandt received about 1,600 guilders for the *Night Watch,* and four years later the Prince of Orange gave him 2,400 for two smaller works.

The fable of the *Night Watch* may owe its stubborn survival to the fact that it is a simple and convenient means of disposing of a complex matter. In 1642 Rembrandt was at the height of his popularity, and thereafter he slowly fell out of public favor, though never to the extent that romantic biographers suggest. What were the reasons for his "decline"? One of them, certainly, was a change in Dutch tastes in art. During the 1640s wealthy citizens, perhaps growing a trifle soft in their security, developed a fondness for showiness and elegance. They began to prefer the bright colors and graceful manner that had been initiated by such painters as the fashionable Flemish portraitist Anthony van Dyck—who, however fine an artist, lacked Rembrandt's depth. Rembrandt's use of chiaroscuro dissatisfied them too, and they turned away from an artist who seemed "dark" and—what was perhaps worse—demanded that they devote some thought to what they were looking at.

Several of Rembrandt's pupils, among them Jacob Backer and Ferdinand Bol, were quick to adapt themselves to the new taste for elegant, highly finished pictures and soon began to receive richer commissions than their master. There is no evidence that Rembrandt ever expressed the slightest resentment of this; indeed, it is said that he freely lent his studio props to others who made more money than he did. But he would not make concessions in his art, even though his need for money grew increasingly acute. On the contrary, while the new vogue indicated where the financial future lay, his work became steadily quieter and more profound. Not many Dutch connoisseurs were willing to accompany him in that direction; even his early admirer and patron Constantin Huygens lost rapport with him. In the late 1640s, when Huygens was asked by the widowed Princess of Orange to make a list of artists who might decorate Huis ten Bosch ("the house in the woods"), one of the royal residences near The Hague, he included the names of some of Rembrandt's pupils, but not the master himself. And years later, when Rembrandt died, Huygens did not bother to note the fact in his diary, although he frequently made mention of many minor painters.

Frans Banning Cocq, ranking officer of the quasi-military fraternity in Amsterdam that commissioned Rembrandt to paint *Night Watch (pages 82-85),* was apparently so pleased by the result that he had a small watercolor copy of it made for his family album *(below).* The opposite page of the album—still intact after more than 300 years—bears the elegantly penned legend, "The young Captain Banning Cocq ordering his Lieutenant, William van Ruytenburch, to march the company out."

Another reason for Rembrandt's decline in popularity may have been his dedication to Biblical painting. At the outset of his career there had been a fair, if dwindling, market for religious works. But in the mid-1640s Rembrandt stood almost alone among Dutch artists in interpreting the Scriptures. He was primarily a portrait painter—about 400 of his 600 known works are in that category—but many of the portraits are of Christ, the disciples, the prophets and anonymous figures who call to mind the Old and New Testaments. Altogether there are about 160 Biblical paintings, plus 80 etchings and more than 600 drawings. There are few records of commissions for the Biblical paintings; Rembrandt seems to have produced these works to satisfy himself, although perhaps hoping to sell them later. But Dutch buyers of non-commissioned paintings preferred to spend their money for landscapes and genre scenes.

In the auctions of Rembrandt's possessions in 1657 and 1658, a number of his paintings were sold. Apparently they went very cheaply. The prices obtained for individual works are not known, but the total amount realized was pathetically small. Among the auctioned paintings was one described as "one large Descent from the Cross." Today a now priceless work on that theme, dated 1634, is in the Hermitage Museum in Leningrad. If the auctioned work and the Hermitage painting are one and the same, Rembrandt must have had it in his studio for 23 or 24 years without selling it. Like most artists, he kept some of his paintings on hand for extended periods, sometimes as a source of inspiration, sometimes in order to rework them. But it seems unlikely that he would willingly have held one for nearly a quarter of a century—particularly when he was in need of money.

In his religious paintings, during his transition from youthful exuberance to the calm reflectiveness of middle age, Rembrandt became more and more concerned with the inner reactions of the individuals he portrayed than with their outward actions. It was no longer the Biblical stories as narrative, but their meaning for the individuals involved, that attracted him. At about the time of the *Night Watch* he produced the *Sacrifice of Manoah*, a monumental, classically simple painting that clearly reveals his new preoccupation. As Rembrandt depicts the scene, an angel has just appeared to the aged Manoah and his barren wife to tell them that they will become the parents of the hero Samson; at the moment caught in the painting, the angel is departing at upper left. In his earlier years, Rembrandt might have painted Manoah and his wife staring at the apparition, their arms raised in astonishment. But here the old couple kneel in silence, hands quietly clasped in thanksgiving. Their eyes are closed; they do not see the vanishing angel but are wholly absorbed in the meaning, not the manner, of the miracle.

The increasing realization of true human values in Rembrandt's work of the 1640s may have grown out of unhappy personal circumstances: the several deaths in his family, his embroilment with Geertghe Dircx. Such troubles, which might have led him to become bitter, seemed to have the opposite effect. An air of tenderness, a new strength of faith, suffused his art. Re-creating the world of warmth and intimacy that had been temporarily lost to him, he turned repeatedly to the theme of the

Infant Christ; there are a number of works from this time that show the Holy Family and the Flight into Egypt. He filled his paintings with homely details: the Virgin warming her feet at a tiny fire, a cat ready to snatch at the bowl from which the Child has just been fed. Rembrandt was able to place the Holy Family in humble Dutch interiors without violating any sense of decorum. It does not seem anachronistic but perfectly logical to see the Christ Child in the home of a 17th Century Amsterdam carpenter, where the artist devoutly supposed that the Child might indeed be found, at least in spirit.

Rembrandt's deepening perception of life, and his stress upon the simple, tender aspects of it, can be seen in his drawings and etchings of secular subjects as well as in his religious works. In the 1640s he extended and amplified what he had expressed in *The Good Samaritan* of 1633: all things descend from God and are not to be scorned. The Good Samaritan was another theme to which he often returned: around 1648, for example, he used it in two paintings and three drawings. His drawings of street scenes, of pancake sellers, of quacks hawking their dubious wares, and particularly his studies of women and children—some 60 of the latter are known—are full of affection and penetrating observation. His drawings became wonderfully concise: his chalk sketch of *Two Women Teaching a Child to Walk (page 52)* contains an absolute minimum of lines yet perfectly suggests the bent brittleness of a grandmother, the suppleness of a young woman, the awkward anxiety of a child. Either adding to the sketch or subtracting from it would have injured it.

Although Rembrandt often used chalk in his early years, in the 1640s pen and ink became his favorite medium in drawing and remained so. He used the pen directly, seldom bothering to make the preliminary pencil or chalk sketches that other artists found necessary. Indeed, a guideline followed by scholars today in determining the authenticity of the many pen sketches tentatively attributed to Rembrandt is to look for traces of underdrawing beneath the pen strokes. If these are found, the drawings are almost certainly the work of pupils or copyists.

Rembrandt often "drew" with a brush alone—a fact that may well seem a contradiction in terms to those who think of this implement solely in connection with painting. His magnificent *A Woman Sleeping (page 55)*, which is rightly considered among the greatest drawings extant, is executed entirely with a brush; many of its subtleties depend on the weight of the strokes and the amount of liquid Rembrandt permitted the brush to carry.

In other drawings Rembrandt frequently combined brushwork and pen strokes, making his sketch first with the quill or the reed, then applying a wash with the brush. His economy of line and delicacy of touch were long misunderstood by 18th and 19th Century collectors; some owners of his drawings found them "incomplete," and sometimes had further brushwork added with the idea of "finishing" them. More than one great Rembrandt drawing has been ruined by a collector who attempted to "correct" what he supposed had been inadvertence or laziness on the artist's part. It should be noted here that none of the drawings shown on pages 49-60 has been retouched; the reader may be interested in conjecturing how and to what extent he personally might attempt to change them. If there is indeed someone who believes he could "correct" *A Woman Sleeping,* for example, it is to be hoped that he will be able to explain this to Rembrandt van Rijn in the celestial dark alley where they meet.

The third great category of Rembrandt's achievement—his etchings—also reflect the transitional nature of his art in the 1640s. One of his finest prints, *Three Trees (pages 148-149),* remains highly Baroque in its dramatic atmosphere and its strong contrasts of light and dark. In other works he displays a greater breadth of view and an increased calm. Rembrandt spent much time working out of doors in the Dutch countryside near Amsterdam—a number of his small landscapes *(pages 97-103)* can be correlated with scenes that still exist—and he seems to have absorbed these quieter qualities from the natural world; Baroque theatricality does not accord well with the vast stillness of earth and sky. This calmer manner appears in the etching he did in 1645 of *Six's Bridge (page 98).* Here Rembrandt is completely realistic, faithfully recording the broad reach of the land and the luminous, breeze-stirred air.

In all his etchings, Rembrandt worked with great speed. His pace is suggested in an old story, recorded by Edmé François Gersaint, an 18th Century French art dealer who compiled the first catalogue of Rembrandt's etchings. Gersaint could not, of course, have known Rembrandt; moreover, he had a Gallic predilection for collecting gossip. Perhaps, then, the story is only another of the fables that encrust the artist's memory. Still, a glance at *Six's Bridge* indicates that Gersaint may not have been far wrong. "This Plate," he wrote, "was produced by an Incident which deserves to be remembered. It has before been remarked that Rembrandt lived in great Intimacy with the Burgomaster Six and that he was frequently at his Country-Seat. One Day when they were there together, the Servant came to acquaint them that Dinner was ready, and as they were sitting down to Table, they perceived that Mustard was wanting: the Burgomaster immediately ordered his Servant to go into the Village and buy some. Rembrandt, who knew the Slothfulness of Dutch Servants, and that when they answer *anstons* [a-coming], are an Hour before they appear, offered the Burgomaster a Wager that he would etch a Plate before his man returned with the Mustard. Six accepted the Wager, and Rembrandt, who always had Plates at Hand ready varnished, immediately took up one and scratched upon it the landscape which appeared from the Window of the Parlor where they were sitting. The Plate was indeed finished before the Fellow came back, and Rembrandt won his Wager. . . ."

The darting grace and simplicity of the lines of *Six's Bridge* represent only one aspect of Rembrandt's work on copper during this period. On other occasions he used strokes so tiny that they can best be seen with a magnifying glass; he combined literally thousands of them in half-shadows and shadows so rich that they rival those in his own paintings. These minute, closely set lines may be seen in several of his finest works of the time, for example in *Thomas Jacobsz. Haaring (page 151)* and in the portrait masterpiece, *Jan Six, Reading (page 150).*

On rare occasions Rembrandt made illustrations for books written by his friends. This etching was used by Jan Six as the frontispiece to *Medea,* his long play based on Greek myth. It shows Medea hiding behind an altar as Jason—whom she led to the Golden Fleece—betrays her love by marrying another woman. Curiously, Rembrandt chose to illustrate this scene even though it is not part of Six's play.

As he experimented with his etching technique Rembrandt began increasingly to use a "dry point" needle (stronger and heavier than the thin etching needle) with which he scratched directly on his plates, using this device in combination with the lines etched on the plates by acid. By varying the pressure of his strokes he produced both thin lines and thick. The curl or "burr" of copper raised by the dry point needle was left on the plates, not scraped away as in engraving; it retained the printing ink, thus creating strong, velvety accents almost like those of charcoal. In Rembrandt's *Self-Portrait, Drawing at a Window (page 95)* heavy dry point lines are particularly noticeable on his sleeve and around the open throat of his coat.

Often, when he wished to create very delicate layers of shading which could not be produced either by the etching needle or with dry point, Rembrandt used the even thicker engraver's burin as well. All three implements, in what amounts to a whole new style of etching, were used in his most celebrated print, *Christ Healing the Sick (pages 154-157)*, which was probably completed about 1648, although Rembrandt must have worked on it intermittently for at least several years before that. Only 10 impressions of this work—the so-called "Hundred Guilder Print," because of the price one impression reputedly brought—survive from the first state of the complete plate. The soft burr left by the dry point needle was rapidly worn down in the press, and later impressions became increasingly pale until the plate was finally ruined by re-working. The theme in this work is rare in his art—perhaps unique—because he does not limit himself to a single dramatic moment in the life of Christ but instead chooses to combine several episodes in the Biblical text he illustrated.

At the time of the "Hundred Guilder Print" Rembrandt again took up the subject of Christ at Emmaus, which he had first painted about 20 years earlier in Leiden. The 1648 *Emmaus (page 104)* cannot be said to mark a sharp turning point in his career or the end of his middle period and the beginning of his maturity; but it does afford an opportunity to point out, in a single great work, the extent of his development during the preceding eight or nine years. The arrangement of the four figures in the painting has a classical simplicity and symmetry that may very well have come from Leonardo da Vinci's *Last Supper,* although it is in no way imitative. The painting is restrained, hushed, and the luminescence around the head of Christ is far from a sunburst or halo. The divinity is also suggested by a classical device that Rembrandt had by then learned very well how to use: the lofty niche above the figure of the Savior, physically occupying so much of the painting, is a piece of architecture that speaks aloud. Yet Rembrandt differs from Raphael or Michelangelo, who both inspired and repelled him, in that there is nothing occult or physically superhuman in the figure of Christ. Rembrandt presents Him as the Son of Man, who had known suffering and death; His qualities are gentleness, meekness and love. In art there are few, if any, more human representations of Him. The capacity to produce so great a work had been attained by Rembrandt at 42. He was not yet in his "mature" period and fruitful years lay ahead.

Rembrandt's etching of David and Goliath was one of four Old Testament scenes that he illustrated for a book, called *Piedra Gloriosa* ("The Glorious Rock"), by one of his close friends, Rabbi Menasseh ben Israel. Rembrandt, who made his home in Amsterdam's Jewish quarter, was interested in Hebrew theology and probably was intrigued by the Rabbi's work, which developed the mystical theory that the stone David slung at Goliath symbolized the eventual coming of the Messiah and the triumph of Jewish spiritual leadership.

It would require an unreasonable partisan to insist that Rembrandt produced a masterpiece each time he faced his easel. Not many people would rank his portrait of his wife Saskia as the Roman goddess Flora *(page 120)* as one of the imperishable monuments of Western Man. Most museum directors, if they could choose, would forgo it for *Woman Bathing (opposite)*, an intimate oil sketch of his mistress Hendrickje. However, the fact is that in more than 600 paintings Rembrandt's level of excellence was exceedingly high, and, moreover, that his range was wonderfully wide.

While his fame rests largely on his portraits and Biblical paintings, he also dealt with history, mythology and everyday life. Not until early in this century—when the first comprehensive catalogue of his paintings was completed—could admirers appreciate the varied panorama he had set before them. It was, and still is, astonishing to find that the sensuous *Danaë (pages 118-119)* and the heroic *Julius Civilis (pages 126-129)* came from the hand of one man.

If Rembrandt had an identifying hallmark, aside from his technique, it was his personal approach. He did not think in terms of historical epochs or of dated "types"; the unknown model for the "pagan" Homer *(page 124)* appears in other works as an Old Testament patriarch. To Rembrandt, humanity was the supreme concern. It did not matter where or when.

The Breadth of Genius

Rembrandt himself might well have been surprised at the worldwide recognition achieved by this small work, only about 24 by 18 inches. An affectionate gesture toward his faithful mistress, it may also have served as a preliminary study for one of his paintings of the Biblical Bathsheba.

Woman Bathing, 1654

117

Rembrandt's *Danaë* is by far the most beautiful of the few female nudes he painted. But the most striking quality of this work is its light, which relates directly to the myth with which the artist was dealing. According to the story, an oracle warned the Greek king Akrisios that his daughter, Danaë, would bear a son who would kill him. He therefore kept her in enforced chastity, symbolized in the painting by the weeping, fettered cupid at top right. However, the god Zeus, taking the form of a golden shower, evaded her guardian maid servant and entered Danaë's bedchamber; from their union came a son who eventually fulfilled the prophecy. Here Danaë raises her hand, both to shield her eyes and to welcome her arriving lover, whose presence Rembrandt represents in the magnificent, unearthly yellow light pouring voluptuously over her face and body.

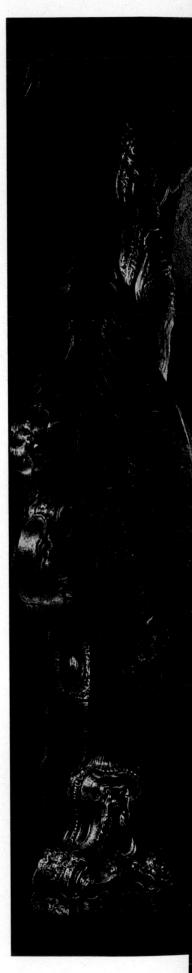

118

Homer, 1663

Supremely gifted with both vision and insight, Rembrandt often turned, paradoxically, to the subject of blindness in his paintings. Perhaps what he wished to say was that one does not need mere visual capability to discern truth. Both the blind *Homer (left)* and the *Aristotle Contemplating the Bust of Homer* were painted in the last two decades of Rembrandt's life. The *Homer* has been damaged, probably by fire—originally the aged poet was

THE METROPOLITAN MUSEUM OF ART, NEW YORK, PURCHASED WITH SPECIAL FUNDS AND GIFTS OF FRIENDS OF THE MUSEUM, 1961

Aristotle Contemplating the Bust of Homer, 1653

pictured in discourse with a scribe and perhaps also a student—but it has weathered the loss. The bard's sightless eyes, his aimlessly groping hands, provide perhaps the most poignant representation of blindness in the entire history of art. In the *Aristotle and Homer* the philosopher's thoughtful face is another of Rembrandt's major triumphs, achieving an expressiveness in paint that few men could emulate in words.

125

Like the last quartets of Beethoven, the late works of Rembrandt are so complex and profound that they are often less appreciated than his earlier works of straightforward power. This is particularly true of an ill-fated and misunderstood painting commissioned by Amsterdam city authorities for the town hall: the now mutilated *Conspiracy of Julius Civilis*. The scene records the start of an uprising in 69 A.D. against Roman domination

Conspiracy of Julius Civilis (sometimes called *Oath of the Batavians)*, fragment, 1661-1662

by barbaric tribesmen, the Batavians, who were ancestors of the Dutch and whose chieftain had adopted a Latin name, Julius Civilis. Rembrandt, painting as though his brushes were dipped in liquid light and fluid shade, created a work that was monumental and at the same time subtle. Tragically, his official patrons failed to understand the painting and rejected it, for reasons that are suggested on the following page.

Drawing for *Conspiracy of Julius Civilis,* 1661

A single word never suffices to interpret a painting, yet in the case of
the *Conspiracy of Julius Civilis* one word—"Shakespearean"—is fairly apt.
With that in mind, the viewer need no longer look for a literal representation
of history; instead, something of the mysterious ambience of *King Lear* or
Macbeth comes to mind—archaic, barbaric, lordly, wild. There is not the
slightest evidence that Rembrandt ever read Shakespeare, but there is every
evidence that the two masters arrived independently at a common view of the
remote, strange past.

Rembrandt's treatment of the historic conspiracy is astonishing: he painted
a time and an emotion more than a particular event. His preparatory sketch for
the work, above, indicates the majesty of his conception. But the men who
ordered the painting were not prepared for the result. They may well have
asked why the face of Julius Civilis was not turned in profile, to hide his
hideous, empty eye socket. They may also have asked why the Batavians—
whom the Dutch were proud to have as ancestors—were not nobly drawn. In
any event, the *Julius Civilis* was removed from the town hall. Rembrandt later
cut down the huge canvas—originally 96 square feet in size—hoping to make
its central group salable, and this remnant is now the prized possession of the
National Museum of Stockholm. There the huge, half-blind Batavian leader
still holds aloft his sword, and the oath of rebellion is forever sworn upon it.

One of the most breathtaking of Rembrandt's late works, the so-called *Jewish Bride,* may have been a commissioned wedding portrait of two members of Amsterdam's community of Sephardic Jews who allowed the artist to represent them as figures from the Old Testament—as Isaac and Rebecca, perhaps, or Ruth and Boaz.

In this painting the artist reveals the immense coloristic power of his final years; the light seems to come from within the figures, almost supernaturally illuminating their faces and garments. In the detail below, Rembrandt's technique of combining heavy paint and thin glazes is particularly apparent. He modeled his forms with thick impasto laid on with a palette knife to a depth of as much as a quarter of an inch. Then, using a small amount of pigment suspended in oil, he repeatedly brushed lightly over the surface, adding the subtlest depths and variation to his colors.

The Jewish Bride, c. 1665

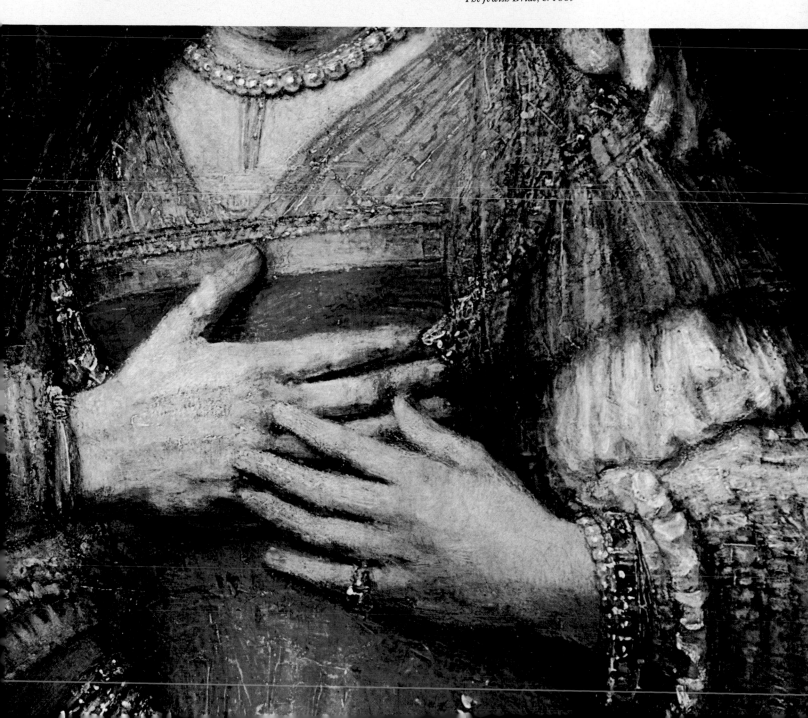

VI

Triumphs
and Trials

The many biographers of Rembrandt, as though they were all members of some worldwide union, seem to follow certain rules in dealing with him. One of these is to announce that in the last two decades of his life—from 1649 to 1669, when he was beset by personal disasters—he lifted his art into the realm of the soul or spirit, soaring where few, if any, other painters have been able to go. This has been said in Dutch, German, English and conceivably Uzbek—and, in fact, it must be said, because it is quite true. However, since "soul" and "spirit" are essentially indefinable words, it requires a roundabout approach to arrive at the heart of the matter.

A beginning can be found in a statement by the English novelist Henry Fielding. In his preface to *Joseph Andrews,* Fielding wrote: "It hath been thought a vast commendation of a painter, to say his figures seem to breathe; but surely it is a much greater and nobler applause, that they appear to think."

In the portraits Rembrandt made as a young man in Amsterdam, his figures *did* seem to breathe, but they did not yet appear to think. Most of these early portraits conveyed an impression of imminent activity rather than of thought. The merchant was about to return to his warehouse, the captain to his ship, without memory or anticipation.

As Rembrandt matured in the 1630s and 1640s, the nature of his portraiture changed; he penetrated deeper, emphasizing the inner state of his subjects and paying less heed to detailed external description. To some of his contemporaries this was disconcerting. The tradition of the Dutch demanded a portrayal of outward reality, and the idea of subordinating this to seek out the more profound reality that lies within man was difficult for them to grasp.

Rembrandt did not alter or distort the appearances of his subjects in order to impose on them his own view of what their "souls" or "spirits" were like. He simply chose to emphasize certain features that seemed to him quintessential. Among his sitters there were several who were also portrayed by other artists. A comparison of the likenesses made by them and by Rembrandt confirms that he was faithful to visual appearances.

In his portrait of Jan Six, later Amsterdam's burgomaster, Rembrandt achieved one of his most searching characterizations. At this very instant Six seems to be turning his gaze from the world outside to a realm within himself.

Portrait of Burgomaster Jan Six, 1654

133

But he took a longer and deeper view, and tempered it with his own sense of humanity. By the time he had attained the height of his power in portraiture, his subjects not only "appeared to think," but also to be listening to inner voices that seemed to whisper to them from beyond the region of thought.

Not all Dutchmen, by any means, objected to Rembrandt's searching characterizations. Some of his greatest portraits are commissions ordered during his last decades, when any sophisticated citizen of Amsterdam would have known that the artist was uninterested in producing a "fashionable," superficial likeness but would probe far beneath the surface. Among those who sat for Rembrandt in the 1650s were his friend Jan Six, later to be Burgomaster of Amsterdam; Ephraim Bonus, a Sephardic physician and writer; Nicolaes Bruyningh, a young aristocrat; and Arnout Tholinx, Inspector of the Medical Colleges of Amsterdam. Others who have been tentatively identified in Rembrandt's paintings were Clement de Jonghe, a publisher of prints, and the Spanish poet Miguel de Barrios. Perhaps by no coincidence, the men who commissioned portraits from Rembrandt during his mature years appear to have had in common, among other qualities that radiate from the canvases, intelligence. It is not likely that he flattered them by deliberately endowing them thus, but rather that their intelligence led them to sit for him.

The portrait of Jan Six (page 132) is one of the most arresting in all art, and has moved sober critics to flights of lyricism in their attempts to grapple with it. The German art historian Carl Neumann, in his perceptive study of Rembrandt, described Six's expression in these words: "This man's mind is full of thoughts. He is about to go out among the people, perhaps to the Town Hall; there pass before him, as in a dream, all those with whom he regularly deals. He listens to their words, and divines also their more secret thoughts and interests. . . . And as all this crowds before him, a reflective, somewhat melancholy smile comes into his eyes; an otherworldly and penetrating look plays over his features. There is a trace, too, of the sympathetic kindness of the detached bystander, forming altogether a complexity of expression which seems inexhaustible, and is not met with in any other portrait in the world."

If Neumann's words "secret" and "otherworldly" are taken together, and their meanings merged into one nameless thing, that thing begins to approximate what Rembrandt strove successfully to express. But it is only a beginning. Jan Six is a leader who goes to the town hall, who has important dealings and who can afford to be a detached if sympathetic bystander. However, there are other men in Rembrandt's world, and our own, who are not in that position. Yet the nameless thing—"spirituality" comes close but does not quite strike the mark—appears in such men too. He makes this very plain in his painting of *Two Negroes* and in his *Man with a Gilt Helmet*; the sitter for this latter picture is traditionally believed to have been his brother Adriaen, who followed his father's trade as a miller.

In Rembrandt's view, it was not necessary to have any special worldly stature—or, for that matter, to be of any particular age—to possess the strange intangible; for it was common to all mankind. He saw it in a boy *(page 88),* and in the philosopher Aristotle *(page 125).* Above all, he saw and felt it in himself; how better, indeed, may an artist grasp it than by looking inward and then, by empathy, realizing it in others? His self-portraits from the late 1640s onward are rich with this profound and mysterious current. But precisely what it is may never be wholly defined. It is simply the quality—secret, otherworldly, spiritual, meditative—that all great religious leaders, and supremely Christ, have tried to touch in the hearts of men.

The artistic means by which Rembrandt captured or suggested this essential quality can at least partially be described. Of particular note is the way in which his sitters glance—or do not glance—at the spectator. Their eyes are not furtively averted, but neither do they stare directly outward. These men are of this world and yet not in it. Gravely dignified, they are engrossed in their own thoughts, remembering and listening, and it was part of Rembrandt's gift to convey that fact by his sheer skill in painting human expressions. But beyond this technical mastery, which other artists have possessed, lay his unmatched ability to use chiaroscuro. Out of the depths of his genius he summoned new ways of presenting light and shadow to create an atmosphere that half conceals and half discloses both the tangible and the intangible, in exactly that region where a glimpse of the "soul" may be caught.

In the self-portraits of Rembrandt's middle and late years *(pages 12, 13)* there are other qualities that relate more particularly to him and to his own circumstances. If in 1640 his face reveals a faintly quizzical expression, in 1650 it displays outright skepticism, not only questioning but also challenging. His look reflects the mood of a 44-year-old man who has passed through melancholy times, but there is a good deal of steel in it: it is the look of one who has searched himself and found his courage undiminished. In 1652, only two years later, Rembrandt appears to have aged considerably. The flesh around his chin has softened, there is a great furrow between his eyes, and the eyes themselves seem to have grown larger. In the 1658 portrait, the eyes are notably luminous, and Rembrandt's expression is one of sadness and vulnerability—with good reason. The impending disaster that he may have sensed in 1650 and 1652 has now overtaken him. By 1658 he has been forced to declare himself insolvent, and the final remnants of his collection of treasured prints and drawings, paintings, curiosities and costumes are in the hands of the auctioneer.

There appears to have been no single calamitous transaction or loss that brought about the tragic collapse of Rembrandt's fortunes. In the 1650s he had fewer commissions than in the 1630s, but he was by no means without patrons. The sales of his etchings continued, and he still had paying pupils. There may not have been a great market for his Biblical or historical paintings, but he had some major commissions—among them *Aristotle Contemplating the Bust of Homer.* Because of the circulation of his prints, his reputation had become international, extending even to Sicily, where it engaged the attention of an aristocratic collector named Don Antonio Ruffo. In 1652 Ruffo wrote to Rembrandt from Messina, commissioning a portrait of "a philosopher," and in 1654 the

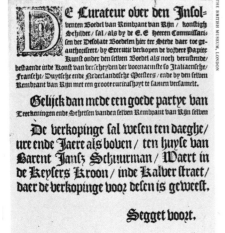

When Rembrandt, in deep financial trouble, declared himself insolvent in 1656, Amsterdam authorities compiled a minutely detailed inventory of his possessions. The first leaf of this document (*above*), lists two plaster casts of children, one plaster head, five works by other artists, four of his own paintings and one shoe. In 1658, a few weeks before the hasty sale of Rembrandt's drawing and print collection, an advertisement (*below*) was circulated that reads: "The trustees of the insolvent property of Rembrandt van Rijn . . . will sell . . . the hereafter mentioned paper art . . . together with a good part of the drawings and sketches of the same Rembrandt van Rijn himself. . . . Pass it on."

DE Curateur ober den Insolbenten Boedel ban Rembrant ban Rijn / konstigh Schilder / sal / als by de E.E Heeren Commissarissen der Desolate Boedelen hier ter Stede daer toe geauthoriseert / by Executie berkopen de bosdere Papier Kunst onder den selben Boedel als noch berustende/ bestaande inde Konst ban berscheyden der boomaemste so Italiaensche/ Fransche/ Duytsche ende Nederlandtsche Meesters / ende by den selben Rembrant ban Rijn met een groote curieushyt te samen bersamelt.

Gelijck dan mede een goede partye ban Teeckeningen ende Schetsen banden selben Rembrant ban Rijn selben

De berkopinge sal wesen ten daeghe/ ure ende Jaere als boven / ten huyse ban Barent Jansz Schuurman / Waert in de Keysers Kroon / inde Kalver straet / daer de berkopinge boor desen is geweest.

Segget boort.

painting of Aristotle and Homer was delivered. The fee is not recorded, but it is known that Ruffo was wealthy and willing to pay more for a Rembrandt than for works by his Italian contemporaries.

In all, it would seem that a prudent painter might have prospered on Rembrandt's income, while even a man of moderately expensive tastes could have avoided catastrophe. But neither frugality nor moderation in financial matters is much mentioned in connection with Rembrandt. His biographer Baldinucci provides an account, possibly distorted but probably correct in essence, of the artist as businessman. Hoping to increase the sales value of his etchings, says Baldinucci, Rembrandt "at intolerable prices . . . had them bought back all over Europe wherever he could find them, at any price." Although a few collectors were delighted to pay large sums for his works on occasion, most were apparently averse to meeting the figures hoped for by the artist, and if Baldinucci's tale is to be believed, Rembrandt's tactic failed. But the real reasons for his ruin were simply that he was a poor manager of his affairs, that he had an almost arrogant disregard for the fair claims of his creditors, and that he was insatiable in amassing his own collections. Like other 17th Century Dutch artists, he also occasionally bought objects for resale but seems to have been none too successful in this regard either.

The actual mechanics of Rembrandt's insolvency are complex and of more interest to accountants and lawyers than to students of art, but at the root of the problem lay the great, handsome millstone of a house which he had purchased in 1639 during his happy, spendthrift years with Saskia. He had bought it for 13,000 guilders but had put down only 1,200 on account. About 15 years later, he had not paid even half of the balance; he had neglected taxes and interest, and still owed 8,470 guilders. He might perhaps have extricated himself from the dilemma by selling the house and moving to smaller quarters, but he was obliged to protect his son's inheritance, which Saskia had entrusted to him. After much maneuvering, he was able to place the house in Titus' name, but his debts remained the same, and he was forced to pledge his personal possessions as security. When his creditors pressed for payment, Rembrandt in 1656 went to the city council of Amsterdam and applied for a *cessio bonorum*—literally, a cession of goods—by which he would agree to surrender his possessions to his creditors. Such recourse was usually permitted to merchants and investors on the basis of "losses at sea or in trade" and was considered less degrading than a declaration of outright bankruptcy. Rembrandt's appeal was granted, but the result was merely a form of facesaving. Although technically he was "insolvent," he was in fact bankrupt.

Legal actions by his creditors dragged on for several years, and it was probably not until 1660 that Rembrandt was forced to move out of his house. Meanwhile, however, the Amsterdam Court of Insolvency inventoried his possessions, and they were sold by a court-appointed bailiff at a number of auctions in 1657 and 1658. Apparently the inventory was made with Rembrandt's full cooperation; he was proud of his collections, which would creditably have filled a small museum. There were 363 lots altogether, including such trivial items as No. 360—six handkerchiefs "at the laundry"—but the entire list is so remarkable, and provides such an insight into Rembrandt as an artist and as a man of his time that it is well worth examining in some detail.

There were about 70 of Rembrandt's own paintings, identified very briefly as: "14. One St. Jerome by Rembrandt. 15. One small painting of hares by the same. 16. One small painting of a hog by the same. . . .60. One small picture of a herdsman and animals by the same." Only a few of these paintings—perhaps 10 of the 70—have been located in the centuries since.

The inventory also lists a large quantity of Rembrandt's drawings and etchings. Merely to read the items involved can cause a 20th Century collector or curator to gasp in envy: "236. One book bound in black leather with the best sketches of Rembrandt. . . .238. Yet another book with all the works of Rembrandt." The latter presumably referred to a complete set of his etchings. Although there are extensive collections of these in the British Museum, the Rijksmuseum in Amsterdam, the Bibliothèque Nationale in Paris and the Morgan Library in New York, it is highly doubtful that a complete set can ever be assembled by any museum at any price.

Rembrandt's interest in the work of some of his contemporaries is also manifest in the inventory. Adriaen Brouwer, a painter of low life and peasant scenes, was represented by seven pictures and a book of drawings, and there were works by Rembrandt's teacher Lastman, his friend Lievens, Hercules Seghers, whose landscapes Rembrandt admired, and Jan Porcellis, who specialized in marine pictures. There was also a painting of two dogs by Titus van Rijn, who as a youth must have tried to follow in his father's path. (The painting has been lost, but some surviving drawings attributed to Titus indicate that he had no marked skill. Apparently he abandoned the profession before his death at 27.)

Among the entries in the inventory that require explanation today is "86. One portrait of a dead man by Abraham Vinck." Vinck, a German, worked in Amsterdam early in the 17th Century, when it was a fashion not only to make death masks, but also quickly to paint portraits of the deceased. Item 142, "One child pissing," was probably a small statue. The earthy Netherlanders took delight in matters that others found vulgar, and such statues were occasionally seen as fountains in gardens and even in public squares. One famous example was set up in the city of Brussels in 1619; a replica of it is still there, near the town hall.

Rembrandt's collection of sculpture—most were probably plaster casts rather than originals—included statues of the Roman emperors Augustus and Tiberius, and numerous busts of other emperors, classical heroes and philosophers. (Interestingly enough, the busts of the emperors had been arranged by Rembrandt, the supposed ignoramus, in chronological order in his gallery.) Item 345, with the startling listing "One little child by Michelangelo," was probably another cast, and may well have been copied from the great Italian's Madonna and Child sculpture in the Church of Notre Dame in Bruges, commissioned by a wealthy Flemish family a century and a half earlier.

Rembrandt's collection of Renaissance art included paintings ascribed to Raphael, Palma Vecchio, Jacopo Bassano and Giorgione. There can be no way of verifying these ambitious attributions, but he also had an outstanding collection of prints after Michelangelo, Leonardo, Raphael, Titian, Holbein and Rubens.

Although works of art comprise the bulk of the inventory, there are many other items that suggest the range of Rembrandt's interests. They include: "Two globes. One box full of minerals. Forty-seven specimens of land and sea creatures, and things of that sort. One hand gun and one pistol. Several walking sticks. One arbalest. Several rare cups in Venetian glass. One large lump of white coral. One East Indian basket full of casts and heads. One drawer in which there is a bird of Paradise and six fans. Thirty-three pieces of ancient hand weapons, arrows, staffs, assegais and bows. Thirteen pieces of bamboo wind instruments and fifes. A collection of stags' horns. Five old helmets and shields. One small metal cannon. One [pair of] costumes for an Indian man and woman. The skins of a lion and a lioness, with two colored coats."

Rembrandt had a very small library. One item mentions "Fifteen books of various sizes," without indicating what they may have been. "A book in high Dutch [German] with military subjects" is also listed, as are an old Bible, a German edition of *The Jewish War* by the First Century historian Flavius Josephus, and "Albrecht Dürer's book on proportion with woodcuts." Otherwise Rembrandt, at least at the time of the inventory, appears to have owned no literary works except a copy of *Medea,* an adaptation by Jan Six of the celebrated classical drama. The artist etched the frontispiece for the first edition of his friend's opus, but for some reason chose to depict an incident that does not occur in the play.

Rembrandt's collections were appraised at more than 17,000 guilders. However, only about 5,000 guilders were realized in the sales, leaving him still heavily in debt. The low prices may be attributed both to the falling off of his popularity and to an economic depression of the time; the Dutch had lately suffered severe losses in a war with England. But in at least one instance, Rembrandt's fellow-artists in the Guild of St. Luke evidently conspired against him. When a collection of "paper art"— drawings and etchings—was about to go under the hammer, Guild members, fearing that the sudden release of so voluminous and rich a stock might depress the market, arranged for the sale to be hastily held. Before connoisseurs were aware of it, a mass of prints and drawings— Italian, French and Rembrandt's own—was placed on the block, and it fetched the ludicrous sum of 600 guilders.

When the sale of Rembrandt's house finally compelled him to leave it in 1660, he moved, with Titus, Hendrickje and his young illegitimate daughter Cornelia, to a modest rented dwelling in a section of Amsterdam beyond the outermost of the city's three great canals. No doubt the rent was cheap, but it is likely that Rembrandt chose to live away from the center of the city with another reason in mind: after his unhappy experiences, he seems to have been more than willing to withdraw from society. However, he certainly was not—as the myth would have him— without friends. It is true that a number of men (including Jan Six) abruptly disappeared from his life after the "disgraceful" bankruptcy, but others remained loyal. One was a poet named Jeremias de Decker, who must have had Rembrandt in mind when he wrote these lines:

As luck or money runs out, though virtue may still stand,
So friendship straightway falls with her nose in the sand.
I could tell many a tale about that.

In 1666 Rembrandt painted de Decker's portrait—not for money, according to the sitter's story, but for friendship and the love of art. As may be surmised from its late date, the painting penetrated to the man's core. A few of Rembrandt's contemporaries grasped the artist's intent. One of them, another poet named Jan van Petersom, studied the picture and wrote: "O Rembrandt, by your zeal you paint de Decker so that his soul shines through his face. . . ."

There were other friends who stood by Rembrandt and who would, indeed, assume the guardianship of his daughter after his death. Some of his former pupils, too, remained devoted to him. One was Aert de Gelder, who survived him by many years, living well into the 18th Century. Alone among Dutch artists, de Gelder continued to paint in the master's mature style until his own death. His respect for Rembrandt was so great that when he painted a portrait (possibly of himself) as late as 40 years after his apprenticeship, he chose to picture the sitter with Rembrandt's "Hundred Guilder Print" in his hand. Although it would be incorrect to say that Rembrandt was surrounded by a host of affectionate admirers in his final years, he had as many friends as he wished to have and was not destined to go to his grave unmourned or unremembered.

Nor did he—again, contrary to myth—languish in poverty after his bankruptcy. Legally he was obliged to turn over to his creditors any money he might receive from future sales of his art, but an ingenious if not altogether admirable means was found to circumvent the law. (Some of Rembrandt's creditors were kindly men who had made loans to him in his adversity, and who deserved to be repaid.) In 1658 Hendrickje and Titus, then 17, formed a dummy corporation, setting themselves up as dealers in art, and hired Rembrandt as their adviser. While his creditors fumed in frustration, the two "dealers" collected whatever money Rembrandt acquired and passed it to him as "salary." Moreover, Rembrandt—his passion for collecting undimmed—actually resumed his purchases of works of art, although on a much smaller scale than in the past.

The resumption of collecting was only a small sign of Rembrandt's resilience. He also continued to work steadfastly at his art, through all of the disasters of the 1650s and through even worse personal losses that were to follow in the next decade. Portraiture continued to be a major preoccupation. It seems safe to assume that he might have made more commissioned portraits if he had been asked, although it is also easy to imagine him crustily rejecting requests from people whom he did not happen to like. As it developed, most of his paintings were of people whom he asked to pose and who probably paid him little or nothing.

In selecting his sitters, Rembrandt showed no interest in faces that had some obviously striking quality—beauty or ugliness—that might appeal to a modern candid photographer. Instead he sought out individuals in

Rembrandt was fascinated by exotic costumes and personalities. In 1638, perhaps at a carnival, he sketched two elegantly dressed Negro kettle-drummers on horseback (*above*). Two decades later the artist was still interested; this time he copied an Indian miniature painting showing the contemporary Emperor of India, Shah Jahan, in riding attire, practicing falconry. It was Shah Jahan who built the Taj Mahal as a mausoleum for his wife.

whom he could see intimations of the "soul" beneath the flesh. Within the small compass of the human face, Rembrandt tried, more than any artist who has ever lived, to express all that he sensed about God and man—suffering, endurance, love, redemption, even history. Another artist might have chosen to invent faces and expressions that served his purpose, but Rembrandt was too involved with mankind for that. In his late non-commissioned portraits, where preserving a likeness was not an obligation, he may, indeed, have departed from outward reality to spiritualize or ennoble his subjects, making them timeless, transcendental types who might have been encountered in the days of King Saul, in the 17th Century—or last week. But he portrayed the faces of living men.

In these self-chosen subjects, Rembrandt crossed the line between secular and religious portraiture; the men he encountered in the street and invited into his studio were also the saints he visualized in his reading of the Bible. Rubens, in painting a series of apostles, had tried to suggest their strength of spirit by idealizing them—as Michelangelo and Raphael had done before him—as handsome and physically powerful beings. But Rembrandt, who knew his Bible and was his own judge of the qualities of man, saw the apostles and other saints as ordinary mortals, rugged, poor, wrinkled, who had been transfigured by their religious experiences. In 1661 alone he painted five portraits of apostles, using unknown models he had selected, and although some are patriarchal in appearance, not one is a superhuman type. His portrayal of St. Bartholomew, for example, shows a somewhat unattractive, crude man who bears no resemblance to the conventional saintly conception—a fact that caused some ridiculous misunderstandings in the 18th and 19th Centuries.

Rembrandt's intention in this work is plain enough: here is a man of low degree who has seen the light of the Lord and who sits rapt in reflection, pondering this miracle. Like other saints who are pictured with their customary attributes—St. Peter with his keys, St. Paul with his sword—St. Bartholomew is shown holding a knife, recalling the tradition that he was martyred by being flayed alive. About 100 years after Rembrandt made the painting, an English artist, Charles Phillips, produced a mezzotint copy of it. Although the copy is a faithful one, Phillips seems to have doubted that Rembrandt would have painted an apostle with such homely features. In any event, he misinterpreted the symbolism of the knife and titled his mezzotint "The Assassin." In the 19th Century some scholars became dissatisfied with that name and thereupon re-titled the picture "Rembrandt's Cook." The idea that the artist might have employed a chef in 1661, after his bankruptcy, would have startled both Rembrandt and his creditors; but even this re-titling was not the end of the misunderstanding. As late as 1893 an eminent French critic seriously advanced the idea that the portrait was not of a cook at all but of a surgeon. Not until the 20th Century was the matter of identity at last straightened out.

The freedom that Rembrandt enjoyed with the sitters he chose himself —freedom to cast them in such roles as he wished and to dress them in rich costumes—was usually not possible in his commissioned work. Occasionally, however, he was able to find patrons who were sufficiently enlightened and appreciative of his art to allow him a good deal of liberty. This was apparently the case in the so-called *Jewish Bride (pages 130-131)*, a work painted a few years before his death. It appears to be the wedding portrait of a Sephardic couple; the reciprocal admiration between Rembrandt and members of Amsterdam's Jewish community may account for the couple's willingness to be portrayed as they were. There is a deep, Biblical solemnity in the gesture of the man as he places his hand on his wife's breast, a summing-up of the spiritual, emotional and physical aspects of marriage. Rembrandt seems to be portraying the couple in the guise of Old Testament figures—perhaps Ruth and Boaz, Isaac and Rebecca or Jacob and Rachel. Critics continue to advance new speculations as to the real identity of these figures, but even if one were able to settle the question, it would make scant difference. The double portrait speaks for itself. It is one more brilliant example of Rembrandt's ability to combine the worldly and the spiritual.

Rembrandt's fall from fiscal grace did not preclude a number of commissions from even the most sober of businessmen. In 1661 or 1662, about 20 years after the supposed debacle of the *Night Watch* had "ruined" him, according to the myth, he won an important assignment from the Syndics of the Drapers' Guild—in modern terms, roughly equivalent to the officers of a textile manufacturers' association. In response, he produced what is without doubt the greatest of all his group portraits *(pages 86-87)*.

The *Syndics* shows the five guild officers with a servant standing behind them. The traditional interpretation of the painting has been that they are portrayed in the act of making a financial report to the membership in the auditorium. However, recent scholarly research indicates that such public reports were not customary. Why, then, do the Syndics—who are all looking at one point—appear to be responding to some disturbance in their audience? In fact, they are not: there is no audience. Rembrandt has chosen to give his group portrait a touch of drama by having his subjects glance not at someone in an imaginary assembly, but at the entering spectator. The device both unifies the group and adds animation to the picture without detracting from the brilliant characterization of the individuals.

Examinations of the painting by X-ray show how Rembrandt struggled to keep the picture in balance. He shifted all the figures; the servant was moved three times before the artist was satisfied. The finished work has an unshakable stability, subtly maintained by three dominant horizontals: the edge of the table, the level of the heads and the line of the wainscoting. In this framework Rembrandt placed the faces of the men —businesslike, even calculating, but still aware not only of the auditor of ledgers but also of the Auditor of their souls.

After his past experiences with businessmen, Rembrandt may have had reason to be cool or even bitter in his painting, but he was not. His analysis of character transcends all petty feeling. If he discerned self-interest, he saw decency as well; if he saw self-righteousness, he also sensed the rectitude and boldness that obliges men of this century, as well of the 17th, to salute the Dutch.

The Bite of the Print

For Europeans of Rembrandt's day, a print—etching, engraving or woodcut—filled a need that today is met jointly by a work of art and a news photograph. It gave them esthetic enjoyment and also satisfied their curiosity about distant places and people; it was, other than the printed word itself, the 17th Century's major means of mass communication. Publishers—and artists themselves —issued and circulated quantities of prints. Some took the form of simple broadsheets; others illustrated books; others reproduced privately owned paintings inaccessible to public view.

Thus Rembrandt's fame while he lived was greater as an etcher than as a painter (he did no engravings or woodcuts). The acknowledged master of the medium, he turned it into a wondrously flexible instrument of his art. Biblical themes, genre, landscapes, portraits, nudes—all these he found suitable for etching. As much in command of tools as of technique, Rembrandt sometimes employed even the V-shaped engraver's burin in his etchings, combining it with the fine etching needle and thicker dry point needle, as in the work opposite, for richer pictorial effects.

Above all Rembrandt's great gift as an etcher lay in preserving a sense of spontaneity while scrupulously attending to close detail. For him each etching, as the scholar K. G. Boon noted, "originated . . . in the deeply felt need to make that particular print."

Shown in its actual size, this detail from *The Three Crosses (page 145)* provides an indication of Rembrandt's skill at markedly enlarging the dimensions of an etched work without sacrificing any intimacy of gesture or of facial expression.

The Three Crosses, detail

142

The Three Crosses, third state, 1653

In etching a plate, Rembrandt often made changes as he went along, pulling prints of these variations, called "states." The third and fourth states of *The Three Crosses,* shown in less than half their true size, appear above and opposite, respectively. Rembrandt took his text from Luke 23: "And . . . there was a darkness over all the earth. . . . And the sun was darkened, and the veil of the temple was rent in the midst." In the third state the two thieves

THE METROPOLITAN MUSEUM OF ART, NEW YORK, GIFT OF FELIX M. WARBURG AND HIS FAMILY, 1941

The Three Crosses, fourth state, 1653

who were crucified with Christ are clearly seen, as is the Roman soldier who was overcome with revelation and fell to his knees in worship. In the foreground are the "rulers" who had come to vilify Christ; to His right is the Virgin, fainting; behind her St. John stands in a posture of desolation.

In the fourth state, Rembrandt greatly altered his composition, burnishing out several figures and adding others. But the most significant change is in the illumination: now the "darkness over all the earth" has deepened. The supernatural light descending upon Christ has diminished, and the thief at right can scarcely be detected in the gloom. Although each state of the print has its passionate admirers, many prefer the fourth; here the artist's conception of the meaning of Christ's death is realized with overwhelming power.

145

In his etchings of everyday life, Rembrandt moved from a youthful zest for the comical and picturesque to a more mature interest in the essential characteristics of every human being. The three etchings on this page were all made before he was 30. In the *Pancake Woman (left)* one can sense his amusement at the plight of the little girl trying to keep a dog from stealing the treasure she has bought. *The Quacksalver* hawking his nostrums *(below, left)* and *The Ratkiller* peddling his services to a householder *(directly below)* are trenchant commentaries on two seamy Dutch types. The prints opposite—the *Giving of Alms (top)* and *Jews in a Synagogue (bottom)*— date from 1648, when Rembrandt was 42, and reveal his concern with what he had come to find of greater import: the human qualities of kindness and humility, and the reflectiveness of old age.

Pancake Woman, 1635

The Quacksalver, 1635

The Ratkiller, 1632

Giving of Alms, 1648

Jews in a Synagogue, 1648

147

Three Trees, 1643

Rembrandt etched the *Three Trees (opposite, top)* a year after he had completed the *Night Watch*, and it contains much of the Baroque quality of that painting; at this period of his career he seems to have been particularly inclined toward the use of swirling action and color. Ordinarily the words "action" and "color" would appear to be inappropriate in connection with a landscape in black and white, but in this case they are apt enough. While the principal motif of the work is the clump of trees, touched with light and shadow, their massed foliage interpenetrating, the etching is alive with sunshine and storm, and with wind that sends the clouds flying. The scene teems with human activity as well. In the detail below, reproduced here at twice the actual size, lovers loll almost concealed in the foreground bushes; an artist sketches; a man fishes; in the distance farmers move about the plain; and at right a carriage laden with passengers labors up the hill. In its pictorial richness the *Three Trees* does, indeed, rival the most accomplished of Rembrandt's landscape paintings.

Jan Six, Reading, 1647

150

Thomas Jacobsz. Haaring, 1656

Jan Six, *Reading (opposite)* and *Thomas Jacobsz. Haaring* are among the finest of Rembrandt's etched portraits. Both were, moreover, commissioned works; more often paying customers preferred to be depicted in paint. In his study of Six Rembrandt combined genre and portraiture. The sitter's face, lightly etched, tells less about him than do the minutiae of his surroundings; it is the manuscripts, the picture, and the old weapons that stamp him as a scholar, writer and wealthy collector. The study of Haaring is devoid of such details, but no less interesting a portrayal. He was bailiff of the Amsterdam Court of Insolvency at the time of Rembrandt's financial collapse. The artist must have liked the old man nonetheless, for he rendered his face with complete sympathy.

Nude Seated on a Mound, c. 1631

In his reaction against the incredibly perfect nudes of Renaissance art, Rembrandt undertook to show what a naked Dutchwoman really looked like. In this case he may have made his point a trifle too strongly and perhaps unfairly; the woman may not have been merely overfed, but pregnant too. Curiously, it was only after Rembrandt's death that critics took him to task for creating such figures and for revealing such details as the dent left by garters on flesh. In Rembrandt's own lifetime the print met with such success that it was soon copied by another artist to satisfy the demand for it.

The classical proprieties were also Rembrandt's target in *The Good Samaritan (opposite)*. The human figures are not idealized, and the posture of the dog is all too frankly realistic. Some well-meaning Rembrandt partisans have tried to establish that the animal was added by another hand, but the artist was clearly taking a swipe at those prissy people who preferred to avoid confronting the embarrassing crudities that existed not only in the Biblical world but in their own as well.

The Good Samaritan, 1633

153

Shown actual size, *Christ Healing the Sick* (called the "Hundred Guilder Print" for the price it reportedly fetched) combines several episodes from Matthew 19: the healing of the sick *(right)*; the Pharisees arguing *(left)*; the rich young man *(left, hand on face)* who is told to give his money to the poor.

Rembrandt beautifully conveys his conception of Christ as among the people and yet remote from them by making Him slightly taller than the others—although not heroic in stature—and by the use of gesture. Christ's raised left hand sums up the spirit of verse 14 ("Suffer little children . . . to come unto me"). His right hand gently "rebukes" the bald St. Peter *(center)*, who is attempting to bar the approach of a woman carrying an infant.

The detail on the next pages, enlarged five times, shows the artist's decisive placement of each stroke to achieve the sharpness of characterization which helps make this the most famous of all Rembrandt etchings.

Christ with the Sick around Him, Receiving Little Children (Christ Healing the Sick), c. 1648-1650

158

VII

The Last
Full Measure

In the final 20 years of his life, bludgeoned by tragedies that might have crushed a weaker man, Rembrandt achieved a power in his art that has never been matched. The last full measure of his creativity can be felt not only in his religious works and in his portraits but also in such remarkable still lifes as *The Slaughtered Ox (opposite)*. The subject once repelled many people; about a century ago, agents of the Louvre were able to buy the painting at auction for the relatively minor sum of 5,000 francs because no other museums or collectors cared to compete for it.

Today *The Slaughtered Ox* upsets no one, except perhaps those who covet it yet cannot purchase it at any price now. The picture has the magical combination of realism and mystery that is uniquely Rembrandt's. The left side of the ox is not sharply outlined but subtly blended into shadow, and in that regard it is revealing to read the comments of Professor Emeritus Jakob Rosenberg of Harvard in his classic study of the artist, *Rembrandt—Life and Work*. Rosenberg makes the point that Rembrandt always put truth before beauty—"not only the obvious, visual truth of the physical world, but also, penetrating and conditioning it, the spiritual truth." Rembrandt, Rosenberg writes, conceived of both man and nature as "dependent upon the Supreme Force that brought them into being. . . . They are tied up with the creative process of all earthly life. . . . There is no such thing, for him, as *nature morte*. Dead peacocks are combined in his still-life paintings with living persons. Rembrandt is unwilling to cut off anything from the continuous stream of creation— even a carcass, as . . . in his *Slaughtered Ox*. . . . Forms, in his compositions, are not allowed to become too definite or to have any finality, since this would break their contact with the life process."

Because his belief in a "Supreme Force" was so central to Rembrandt's art, the question of his religion itself merits examination. He was certainly a Protestant—but where within that broad category did he find a place? His parents were married in the Dutch Reformed Church, which took its austere theology from John Calvin. Rembrandt was brought up in that church; his four children by Saskia were baptized in it, and there is much in his art that reflects Calvinist attitudes—particularly the view

Reverencing all of God's creatures, Rembrandt saw nothing unseemly in painting this gory ox carcass rather than the more usual subjects of Dutch still lifes. The woman in the background may be the butcher's wife.

The Slaughtered Ox, 1655

that religion touches every area of life, and that man is totally helpless before God. But Calvin's strictness of dogma and his rationality seem not to have had much appeal for Rembrandt, who was emotional, intuitive and no more inclined to follow a rigid system in religion than in painting. Thus, although almost all the official records place him within the Reformed Church, it is likely that he also had another spiritual affiliation.

In the archives of the Reformed Church for 1654 there are four entries relating to Rembrandt, although only the first mentions him by name. The Church Council of Amsterdam, scandalized at the arrangement between Rembrandt and Hendrickje, summoned both of them to account. Hendrickje was living, as the Council bluntly put it, *in Hoererij*—literally in whoredom—with the artist, and had borne him two illegitimate children (one of whom had died). Nothing ensued from the first summons, so three more were issued, but in these only Hendrickje was called. Ultimately she appeared before the Council and was admonished and banned from the sacraments. The ban was lifted when she presented her child for baptism. In the traditional Calvinist view, it is vital to baptize infants as soon as practicable after birth; unbaptized children are believed to be full of the seeds of evil.

Why was Rembrandt ignored after the first summons? Probably the Council discovered that he was not at that time a member of the Reformed Church, and hence was beyond its jurisdiction. In his maturity Rembrandt had turned away from Calvinism in a direction that is indicated by his biographer Baldinucci. Himself a Catholic priest in the days of the Counter Reformation, Baldinucci was disinclined to speak well of any form of Protestantism, but in this case he was fairly gentle. Rembrandt, wrote Baldinucci, professed "the religion of the *Menisti* [Mennonites], which, though false too, is yet opposed to that of Calvin. . . . They do not elect educated preachers but employ for such posts men of humble condition as long as they are esteemed by them honorable and just people, and for the rest they live following their caprice."

The Mennonites take their name and creed from Menno Simons, a 16th Century Dutch theologian who rejected all dogmas, sacraments and ceremonies that were not instituted by Christ or by the Apostles at His order. Menno's followers interpret the Sermon on the Mount literally—and for so doing they have suffered a good deal of persecution. They refuse to bear arms or swear an oath; they oppose any infringement by the state on their freedom of conscience and have even rejected such materialistic practices as insurance and the collection of interest on loans. In Rembrandt's time their spiritual concerns centered on Bible reading, silent prayer and the practice of charity. In accordance with Menno's view they found "the poor in spirit" preferable to "the worldly wise and learned," and drew no social distinctions among themselves. What seemed most important to them in the Sermon on the Mount was the injunction to love thy neighbor. In their theology the emphasis was on Christ as the healer and teacher of men rather than on the formidable God of Calvin.

The simplicity, humility and liberalism of the Mennonites must have appealed powerfully to a man of Rembrandt's nature—and these characteristics are at their most prominent in his last and greatest works. There is no evidence that he actually joined the sect: its members would not have approved of his love of rich costume and his taste for the romantic, and they would have been disturbed even more than the Calvinists by his domestic affairs. But his strongest spiritual affinity in his later years was with the Mennonites. Beyond that, he seems to have lived on the fringes of organized religion, reading and interpreting the Bible in his own highly personal way. And so thoroughly did he read the Bible that of all artists in the Western tradition he has been its most complete "illustrator." So-called Rembrandt Bibles, with pictures selected from his religious paintings, etchings and drawings—more than 800 in all—have been published both in Europe and the U.S. They contain illustrations of almost every book in the Old Testament and the New. Most artists who have essayed this task have confined themselves wholly or largely to one Testament or the other; the "Raphael Bible," for example, focuses on the Old Testament, with only a half-dozen pictures of the life of Christ to illustrate the New.

Whether because of the Mennonite influence or his own deepening conceptions or both, Rembrandt painted no fewer than 11 "portraits" of Christ in the years between 1648 and 1661. All of them emphasize the tender, human aspect of the Saviour and are so similar in general appearance that the same model may have served for all. It is believed that his model was a young Jew, whose own portrait Rembrandt painted from life in 1661; the sitter's face in this work bears a notable resemblance to the Saviour's face in the *Christ at Emmaus (page 104)*. Rembrandt seems to have been the first artist to derive his Christ-type from studying the faces of Jews. For centuries painters had been carefully placing on the placard of the Cross above Christ's head the letters I.N.R.I.—Iesus Nazarenus Rex Iudaeorum; but pictorially they had disregarded the meaning—Jesus of Nazareth, King of the Jews. To the mature Rembrandt it was unthinkable to contradict the Bible by endowing Christ with a classic Greek or a Roman or a Nordic face.

Rembrandt was always to retain his tender conception of Christ, but in the mid-1650s a somber tone began to emerge in his religious art—probably because of a growing tendency to interpret the Bible in the light of his private calamities. As early as 1653, when financial disaster began to loom, the new tragic mood can be seen in *The Three Crosses (pages 143-145)*. In this large etching the emphasis falls on the dark drama on the hill of Golgotha and on Christ's suffering. As Rembrandt worked on his monumental plate, he produced separate states of it, and by the fourth state had transformed his original scene into one of blackening gloom. Although the work is filled with a sense of tremendous affirmation—as one critic has put it, "the Crucifix soars triumphantly into the light like the 'Hallelujah' at the end of a great Baroque oratorio" —it is above all the terrible, final ordeal of Christ that concerns the artist, far more deeply than in any of his earlier Crucifixion scenes.

The same tragic spirit may be detected in the painting of *Bathsheba (pages 172-173)* of 1654—the year in which the Council of the Reformed Church disciplined Hendrickje. It was she who served as the

The bizarre hat perched like a giant cupcake on the head of Gian Francesco Gonzaga, the Italian princeling depicted on this 15th Century lead medal, was the inspiration for the similar creation at the extreme left of Rembrandt's *Three Crosses (page 143)*. Such commemorative or decorative medals were popular collector's items in Rembrandt's day, and it is likely that he or one of his friends owned this one.

THE BRITISH MUSEUM, LONDON

model for Bathsheba, and Rembrandt's rendering resulted in one of the finest nudes of the Baroque era; Rubens may have surpassed it in painting sheer feminine beauty, but no painter equaled it in expression of thought and feeling. In fact very few nudes, in any period of art, can be said to be particularly thoughtful. Botticelli's Venus on her scallop shell seems not to have a brain in her head; Fragonard's *Bathers* are wonderfully ornamental, but one shudders to think what any of them, could she speak, might say; and the odalisques of Ingres give no more promise. But Rembrandt's *Bathsheba* broods poignantly on her situation; she is full of conflicting impulses, well aware of the web of fate in which she is caught and of the tragedy that King David's desire for her will bring.

Biblical figures of stature far greater than Bathsheba's concerned Rembrandt in his final decade, and what seemed to fascinate him most about them was their hours of trial. He came to understand them in the way that one man, having tasted a drop of gall, may understand what it is to drink the full cup. No vanity was involved in identifying his plight with theirs or in inserting his face in scenes of the Crucifixion. Indeed, this was a reflection of Dutch piety of the time, perhaps best expressed by the contemporary theologian Jacobus Revius in a famous sonnet containing these lines:

> *It was not the Jews, Lord Jesus, who crucified You . . .*
> *It is I, O Lord, it is I who have done that to You.*

Steeped in the sadness and frailties of his own world, Rembrandt moved with great insight in the world of the Scriptures. In his *Denial of St. Peter* he portrays a tragically doomed man—not a condemned one, for he will be redeemed, but doomed to break and to reveal his human weakness in his time of trial. In Peter's face, illuminated by a candle held up by a servant girl, the conflict that racks him is expressed with overpowering force: innocence contends with guilt, loyalty with fear. In the distance, Christ, looking back over His shoulder, knows that Peter will deny Him, exactly as He had prophesied. But the painting does more than merely illustrate the Biblical incident. Any man in any century can look at it and ask what ideal, what promise, he is himself about to betray.

In *Saul and David (pages 174-175)* the somberness that filled much of Rembrandt's late religious art is again apparent. The mighty king, who has lost favor in God's sight, tries to find solace in the music of young David—but even as he wipes a tear from his eye, madness and violence boil within him. Saul still wears the trappings of majesty; in the words of I Samuel, 9, "There was not among the children of Israel a goodlier person than he: from his shoulder and upward he was higher than any of the people." Yet Saul's end is not far off, and he will die a suicide. The deep blacks of the shadows so portend, and in a superbly prescient stroke Rembrandt partially isolates Saul by the curtain with which he dries his tears. A 20th Century psychiatrist might well find in this a pictorial suggestion that the king's illness was schizophrenia: the "evil spirit" that possessed Saul caused him to vacillate between gentle, repentant lucidity and furious, uncontrolled lunacy.

Not all of Rembrandt's late religious paintings, however, are permeated with gloom. In 1656, the year he was forced into bankruptcy, he produced one of the most tranquil of all his works—*Jacob Blessing the Sons of Joseph*. The painting is shown and discussed on pages 169-171, but an interesting point remains to be made about it. The bed in which the half-blind patriarch lies is startlingly askew; its footposts and headboard have no relation to each other. Obviously Rembrandt, whose observation of reality and accuracy of line can scarcely be faulted, simply did not care about visual truth when he painted this work. He was concerned with darkening the foreground in order to throw his emphasis on the quiet communion of his human figures. It was the fact of their interaction, not the fact of a bed, that engrossed him. Other great artists have similarly ignored "proper drawing" when it suited them to do so. But this is the privilege of genius; absolute mastery is required before one can effectively take leave of literalism.

Rembrandt's late religious paintings are rivaled in their nobility by his portraits and by a few secular works that he undertook in his last years. One of these is the so-called *Polish Rider (pages 122-123)*. It is hard to tell whether this is a portrait, Biblical or history painting, or genre scene. If it must be categorized, perhaps "romance" is the word. As far as is known, this is one of only two equestrian paintings by Rembrandt in his entire career; the other was a commissioned portrait of an Amsterdam merchant. The usual interpretation of the *Polish Rider* is that he epitomizes all Christian warriors; in the 17th Century men still rode east to do battle against the infidel Turks and Tartars. But it is also possible that Rembrandt may have been making a personal statement in the picture. The rider is heavily armed—he carries a bow, arrows, a sword, a dagger and a war hammer—but in his sensitive face there is a look of vulnerability. Rembrandt as an artist was also heavily armed, and he too was vulnerable to "infidels" who could not understand him. This conjecture cannot be carried far, but it is worth noting that in 1658, when his "downfall" was completed by the auction of the last of his precious possessions, he made an etching called *The Phoenix* which also seems to be a personal comment. In the print, a statue of a hero has been toppled from its pedestal, but its place has been taken by the bird of self-resurrection. Perhaps the artist was defiantly saying that he too would endure.

Certainly his independent attitude toward patrons persisted. The Sicilian nobleman and collector, Don Antonio Ruffo, who in 1652 had commissioned the *Aristotle Contemplating the Bust of Homer (page 125)*, acquired two other paintings from Rembrandt in 1661 and 1663—an *Alexander the Great* and a *Homer (page 124)*. Concerning these works, an intriguing series of letters passed between the Sicilian and the artist, and although Rembrandt's part of the correspondence has unhappily vanished, what remains attests to his continued ruggedness of spirit. Ruffo objected to both paintings, complaining that the *Alexander* was only a head, which had been enlarged on four sides to make it a half-length figure. Rembrandt fought back, informing Ruffo that he would be willing to paint the picture again if Ruffo would pay an additional 500 guilders. The Sicilian also found fault with the *Homer:* in his view, it was unfinished. This was a charge that was often to be made by Rembrandt's later critics, and, according to his biographer Houbraken, he had long since

The most ambitious architectural undertaking in Amsterdam during Rembrandt's day was the construction of a new town hall. The old center of government, shown in the drawing above by the architectural painter Pieter Saenredam, was a complex of dilapidated buildings with no unity of design or construction. (Saenredam also sketched a row of gabled houses that stood nearby.) The new town hall—depicted on the gold medal (*below*) that commemorates the dedication in 1655 —was in a strongly classical style. Rembrandt was one of many artists asked to paint pictures for its decoration, but his offering, the *Conspiracy of Julius Civilis*, was replaced by a work of one of his students.

formulated a crushing reply to it, one that has a particularly modern ring. A painting, Rembrandt noted, "is completed when the master has achieved his intention by it."

Eventually Rembrandt did add to the *Homer* for Ruffo; the nature of the changes he made is not known, but it is likely that he made them on his own terms. In any event, the relationship between painter and patron scarcely suffered. In 1669, the year Rembrandt died, Ruffo came through with a handsome order for 189 of his etchings, which Rembrandt selected and shipped himself.

There was a less happy outcome to a commission he undertook closer to home. Late in the 1650s, after the completion of Amsterdam's great Baroque town hall—today the Royal Palace—the city fathers gave thought to the decoration of its huge south gallery and concluded that scenes depicting the revolt of Julius Civilis would be appropriate. Julius was the leader of a Germanic tribe, the Batavians, that had settled during the First Century in the Rhine delta, in the area of what is now the Low Countries. They were allies of the Roman Empire for most of their history. But at one point Julius led a valiant uprising against the overwhelming power of Rome—his exploits are mentioned in the writings of the Roman historian Tacitus—and to this day the Dutch revere him as one of their greatest forebears. In Rembrandt's day Netherlanders occasionally referred to themselves poetically as "Batavians," and gave the name Batavia to the capital of their East Indian colonies. (Since the Dutch withdrawal in the 1940s it has been renamed Djakarta, and is now the capital of the new nation of Indonesia.)

In the south gallery of the Amsterdam town hall there are eight lunettes below the vaulted ceiling. Each of these semi-circular spaces is large enough to accommodate a monumental painting. It was decided to give the commission to one man, who must at that time have been considered the foremost painter in Holland, and who presumably might have been expected to produce large-scale masterpieces rivaling those produced by Rubens for Marie de' Medici of France several decades earlier for the Luxembourg Palace in Paris. And who was the man the Amsterdam officials chose? The trumpets sound, the lights blaze up, and he steps forth: Flinck.

Govaert Flinck is by no means to be discounted; he had been a pupil of Rembrandt and was a good artist. It may seem astonishing that he was once ranked above his master, but that was the case. Indeed, Rembrandt would not have been given any opportunity to paint anything for the town hall had it not been for Flinck's untimely death in 1660. The huge commission was then divided among several artists, including other pupils of Rembrandt, while the master himself was assigned to paint the first of the lunettes. Even this was not necessarily an honor; the series called for a nocturnal scene, and this was deemed suitable to his "dark" manner. In 1662 Rembrandt delivered his colossal *Conspiracy of Julius Civilis (pages 126-129),* the largest painting he ever made—roughly 20 by 18 feet. But the work in all its glorious savagery did not please the city fathers. The next year it was replaced by a second-rate painting on the same subject, which still remains in the town hall, by Rembrandt's pupil

Juriaen Ovens. To Rembrandt, who by that time had become indifferent to public opinion, the affair was perhaps not a crushing blow. It was, rather, a tragedy for art.

By grim coincidence, it happened that while Rembrandt was at work on the *Julius Civilis* his beloved mistress Hendrickje fell ill—just as his wife Saskia had fallen ill years before while he was planning another huge masterpiece, the *Night Watch*. It is likely that both women were victims of tuberculosis. In 1661 Hendrickje went to a notary to make her will and was described by him as "sick in appearance though still on her feet and active."

The importance of Hendrickje to Rembrandt in his late years was incalculable. He had never been a successful manager of his affairs; it was she who protected him from his creditors after his bankruptcy and provided a home in which he could work undisturbed. She served repeatedly as his model; his last, loving portrait of her, made in 1660, when he must have sensed that life was beginning to slip away from her, reveals a woman of great and simple heart. She died in 1663, and in her will she left her pathetic estate to her daughter Cornelia, with the stipulation that if the child should die, her possessions should go to Saskia's son Titus, then 22. The will also speaks directly to the artist; she "friendly asks Rembrandt" to take care of her little girl. And that was Hendrickje, one of the noblest souls ever to serve a troubled genius.

No loss, however great, could prevent Rembrandt from pursuing his art. He no longer produced etchings, and his last drawings seem to have been made at about the time of Hendrickje's death. Paint became his preferred medium, glowing with the richest colors he had ever used, as evidenced in the *Jewish Bride (pages 130-131)*. In his self-portraits he unflinchingly recorded the slow approach of his own death. In one extraordinary picture he turns to face the viewer, laughing as he had laughed long ago in his earliest etched studies of himself. But now it is a laugh that grips the heart, so wonderfully does it express the feeling of an old man who has seen through all the vanities of the world.

Rembrandt was still occasionally visited in his studio by men of rank and renown. Cosimo de' Medici, scion of a family that had patronized art for 200 years, called on Rembrandt in 1667. C. F. Young, in his famous work *The Medici,* could find no kinder words for young Cosimo than that he was "vain, weak, tyrannical, entirely wanting in brains and sunk in superstition and bigotry." One can imagine him mincing foolishly about the artist's workshop. Not surprisingly, he seems to have found nothing that interested him among the paintings Rembrandt had at hand, although he apparently did purchase (perhaps from a dealer) a *Self-Portrait* that is now in the Uffizi in Florence.

Another visitor was Gérard de Lairesse, an artist from Liège, who had his portrait painted by Rembrandt in 1665. Some years later, when Lairesse had become blind, he took to theorizing about art, and produced a book crammed with rules and regulations. "I do not want to deny that I once had a special preference for [Rembrandt's] manner," he wrote, "but at that time I had hardly begun to understand the infallible rules of art. I found it necessary to recant my error and to repudiate his. . . ." Lairesse also noted that because Rembrandt failed to associate with people of noble rank and refined taste, his subjects were sadly bourgeois.

"The infallible rules of art" to which Lairesse referred were the result of the wave of rationalism that swept through Europe late in the 17th Century and culminated in the "Age of Reason" of the 18th. In art, the French Académie Royale de Peinture et de Sculpture was the fountainhead, the home of the law and the prophets. The French tendency to apply reason to all matters—even those that are often unreasoning, such as art—did not reach its peak until well after Rembrandt's death. By about 1700, however, the precepts generated in the Académie were held in very high esteem. It was even thought possible that artists could be assigned numerical grades, and in 1708 a theorist closely associated with the Académie, Roger de Piles, did exactly that. In a celebrated treatise called *Balance des Peintres,* de Piles graded 57 of "the best-known painters." He established four categories—composition, drawing, color and expression—and in each he awarded a grade, from zero to an impossibly perfect 20.

Because de Piles' grading has considerable interest as a reflection of authoritative critical judgments at a time when the memory of Rembrandt was still fresh, it is worth reproducing here in part:

NAME	COMPOSITION	DRAWING	COLOR	EXPRESSION
Albrecht Dürer	8	10	10	8
Andrea del Sarto	12	16	9	8
Le Brun	16	16	8	16
Correggio	13	13	15	12
Giorgione	8	9	18	4
Holbein	9	10	16	13
Leonardo	15	16	4	14
Michelangelo	8	17	4	8
Caravaggio	6	6	16	0
Veronese	15	10	16	3
Poussin	15	17	6	15
Raphael	17	18	12	18
Rembrandt	15	6	17	12
Rubens	18	13	17	17
Tintoretto	15	14	16	4
Titian	12	15	18	6
Van Dyck	15	10	17	13

In this abbreviated table it will be noted that Rembrandt fares quite well, except for his miserable grade of 6 in drawing: his broken outlines counted heavily against him. But overall, de Piles rated Rembrandt 10th in his list of 57, and spared him the ghastly flunking grades given to Michelangelo and Leonardo in color, and the unmentionable grade received by Caravaggio in expression.

If de Piles' table seems amusing today, it should in fairness be pointed out that he and other rationalists were following the trend of their time. De Piles had a high regard for Rembrandt, and in his other writings said so. Other important critics in the half-century after Rembrandt's death almost invariably had kind words for him, although these were constantly tempered by regrets that he did not use enough light and failed to follow "the infallible rules." The cardinal point ignored by Rembrandt's critics concerned the matter of "expression." De Piles used the word but seems to have thought of it only in terms of pose and dramatic facial contortion. The expression of the human spirit, as Rembrandt achieved it, can never be given an arithmetical rank: it involves immeasurable qualities that include but transcend color, drawing and composition. The point need not be labored, but perhaps it is worth looking once more at the portrait of Jan Six *(page 132)*. Is there a modern viewer who would give that painting a grade of only 12 in expression?

The critiques of the rationalists of course meant nothing to Rembrandt; he was in his grave before the "Age of Reason" fully dawned. It is interesting to note that two other towering figures of the 17th Century, John Milton in England and Blaise Pascal in France, also had little use for rationalism as a means of achieving the most important of all aims: an understanding of God and man. In his *Paradise Regained* Milton denounced classical thought and ordered logic as the evil devices of Satan in his efforts to corrupt the truth of Christ. The French philosopher Pascal, although he did not reject reason, observed in his *Pensées* that "the heart has its reasons, which reason does not know. We feel it in a thousand things. . . . It is the heart which experiences God, and not the reason. This, then, is faith: God felt by the heart, not by the reason." Rembrandt, although scarcely an intellectual, had arrived at the same conclusion and, without recourse to words, had stated it in his art.

Before his own death he had a few final appointments with his God. Just as he had been given to witness the onset of doom in Saskia and Hendrickje, he saw it in Titus. His last portrait of his son is full of sad premonition. Titus died in 1663, less than seven months after he had married; a daughter was born to him posthumously. Otherwise, there remained only Rembrandt's illegitimate daughter Cornelia, who went to far-off Java. She had two children, and as the true daughter of her magnificent mother she named them Rembrandt and Hendrickje.

Two decades before his death, Rembrandt made this drawing of Amsterdam's Westerkerk, where he was buried on October 8, 1669. The church, which was built in Rembrandt's time in the new Dutch classical style, was his parish church. Still standing, it also shelters the tombs of Rembrandt's son Titus and his wife.

One of Rembrandt's last paintings is the *Prodigal Son (pages 177-179)*, and it has served many biographers as a convenient endpiece; in it Rembrandt has returned figuratively to God and has found everlasting peace. But in fact there is some question as to whether the artist ever wandered very far from God. In a review of all his works, matched chronologically against the repeated tragedies of his life, it appears that he never made an angry or a bitter statement. He died in 1669 at the age of 63; what his last illness was, no one can say. He was buried on October 8 in the Westerkerk near his last home in Amsterdam, and in his long slumber he lies near Hendrickje, not Saskia, whose grave is in another part of the city. After his death there was found in his studio an unfinished painting: *Simeon in the Temple*. The theme was one that had preoccupied him since his earliest days. There was surely something profoundly moving to him in the story of the old man, described in the second chapter of Luke, who had lived long enough to see Christ, the Light of the world, and who could then cast up his eyes to Heaven and say, "Lord, now lettest thou thy servant depart in peace."

A Man and His Faith

If a particular area of Rembrandt's painting is to be singled out for greatness, it is in the Biblical pictures of his maturity. Although their existence was of course known, these works were not really "discovered" by artists and critics until fairly near the end of the 19th Century. Among the reasons for the belated revelation was a sociological one: with the growing concept of man as an individual rather than as a faceless and inconsequential unit of society, Rembrandt's expression of this idea two centuries earlier took on a new and modern dimension of meaning.

In his late religious works, regardless of their themes, humanity lies always at the core. It was not as stock characters suitable for painting that Saul the king or Bathsheba the beautiful adulteress or the prophetic Jacob captured Rembrandt's imagination. It was rather what these people felt and endured that moved him. He conceived of Biblical figures in terms of individuals known to him, flawed, fallible or suffering as the case happened to be, and he painted them thus. For Rembrandt the Old Testament was not "history in the shade," as John Calvin called it, a mere record of ancient warnings, admonitions and demonstrations of an implacable God. In the artist's view the Scripture was the beginning chapter of a narrative of man's situation, a dramatic and continuing narrative in which Rembrandt saw himself and his contemporaries as vital participants.

In this detail from *Jacob Blessing the Sons of Joseph*, the fingers of Joseph attempt to direct the luminous hand of his aged father, but they prove as powerless as those of a man who tries to move a sunbeam. The Biblical significance of the subtle interplay of hands is made clear on the following pages.

Jacob Blessing the Sons of Joseph, detail

Jacob Blessing the Sons of Joseph, 1656

The story of *Jacob Blessing the Sons of Joseph* is simply told in Genesis 48. Joseph brings his sons Manasseh and Ephraim to be blessed by their dying grandfather, the almost sightless Jacob. According to hitherto immutable custom, Jacob should have used his right hand to bless the first-born boy, Manasseh. Instead the patriarch, enlightened by God, places his hand on the head of the younger boy, the fair-haired Ephraim, who, he foresees, will be greater than his brother and whose "seed shall become a multitude of nations." In the Scriptural text Joseph is described as "displeased" with his father's act; he tries to move Jacob's right hand toward Manasseh's head and even remonstrates with Jacob. But in the painting Joseph does not make a really determined effort to shift the blessing. It is as if he had decided that it was not for man to intervene in mysteries beyond his comprehension; indeed, he wears an air of submission and even approval of what is taking place. His wife Asenath—who is not mentioned in this incident in the Bible—watches the scene with a tender smile. Rembrandt added her to create the atmosphere of a warm family group, and he chose as his predominant colors harmonies of yellows and reds which he often used in his mature years. The artist's message in this lofty pictorialization of a story from the Old Testament seems to be a direct expression of the words of the New: "Thy Will be done."

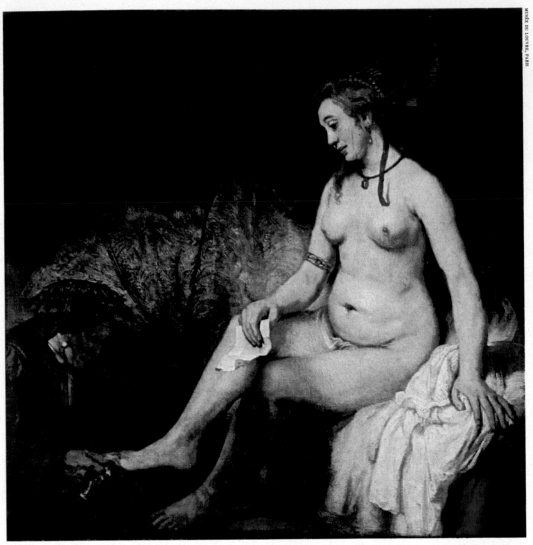

Bathsheba, 1654

The story of David and Bathsheba (II Samuel, 11) had a particular fascination for Rembrandt, who painted it in the 1630s and 1640s, slowly shaping his thoughts for his greatest portrayal of it in 1654. In this conception, Bathsheba has just completed her bath and holds in her hand the newly arrived letter from King David, summoning her to his palace. In her face and in the melancholy tilt of her head (X-rays reveal that Rembrandt made changes in position before achieving precisely the attitude he sought) are summed up the emotions that course through her. There is a sense of loyalty to her absent husband, Uriah; balancing this is her physical desire to share the bed of the great king; and overriding both is her anticipation of the doom that must surely overtake her. Meanwhile the servant, who knows nothing and senses nothing of Bathsheba's turmoil, goes on methodically drying her mistress' feet. Hendrickje was the model for Bathsheba; coincidentally, she bore Rembrandt an illegitimate daughter during the year the painting was completed.

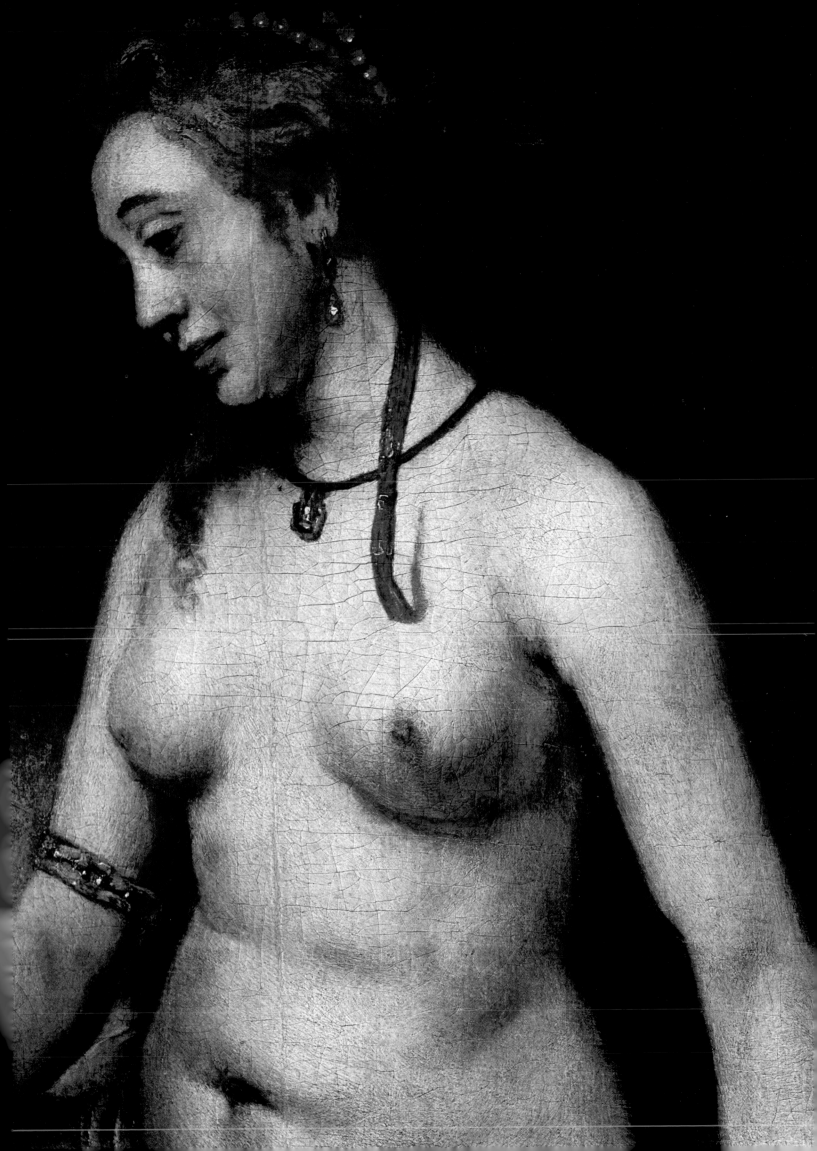

Saul and David, c. 1658

In his late years Rembrandt's religious paintings were often charged with a deep sense of gloom and of awe at the helplessness of men—even the most powerful of them—before God. He in no sense slackened in his religious faith but turned to tragic themes perhaps because of his own experiences. His *Saul and David* shows the old king half-mad with grief because the Lord has withdrawn His favor from him and bestowed it on young David, the shepherd boy who had become Saul's armor-bearer and whose harp-playing soothed the king when the "evil spirit" was upon him. In the eye of the weeping Saul *(detail, opposite)* may be seen the inner struggle that racks him. Love for David is contending with wrath, and we sense that soon the conflict will erupt in a mad attempt at murder. Dark shadows and somber colors intensify the mood of impending explosion; it seems that in another instant Saul's hand, relaxed on his javelin, will clench, and he will hurl the weapon with intent to "smite David even to the wall with it" (I Samuel, 18).

175

David and Uriah, c. 166

As in the case of several of Rembrandt's untitled paintings, the subject of the work above continues to be debated by scholars. Of a number of ideas that have been suggested, the likeliest is that it represents the incident in II Samuel, 11, in which King David *(right)* sends Bathsheba's soldier-husband Uriah *(foreground)* to certain death on the battlefield, his downcast look betraying foreknowledge of his fate.

Return of the Prodigal Son, c. 1669

There can be no doubt, however, about the subject treated above—the return of the Prodigal Son (Luke, 15). This painting constitutes Rembrandt's final statement on the Christian idea of forgiveness and mercy. As the prodigal kneels, his father's expression is consummately gentle, and his embrace *(detail, next pages)* symbolizes Rembrandt's hope for the safe return of all lost and troubled voyagers on the ocean of the world.

177

THE METROPOLITAN MUSEUM OF ART, NEW YORK. BEQUEST OF MICHAEL FRIEDSAM

Bellona, 1633

The brilliance unveiled

The restoration of Rembrandt's paintings has dispelled the centuries-old notion that he painted only in somber tones. This photograph shows a half-cleaned portrait of Saskia, the young Rembrandt's bride-to-be, dressed as Bellona, the Roman goddess of war. The uncleaned left half has a murky amber cast caused by the accumulation of dirt and by at least two layers of tinted varnish applied by well-meaning 19th Century picture restorers to protect the painting. The right half clearly demonstrates, however, that Rembrandt's original work included natural skin tones, brilliant whites and cool greys.

The delicate task of lifting Bellona's veil of varnish fell in 1947 to The Metropolitan Museum of Art in New York City. First, restorers analyzed the coating's chemical make-up and selected a solvent potent enough to dissolve it without injuring the paint beneath. Then, using cotton swabs, they applied the solvent to the canvas a centimeter at a time. When the entire canvas had been cleaned, a signature and date, which had been nearly invisible in the lower left corner, were checked, and the picture, whose authenticity had been doubted by some critics, was proved a genuine early Rembrandt.

Copper plate for etching: *Giving of Alms*, 1648

The lost recovered

In 1956 the art world was stunned by the news that a fabulous cache of Rembrandt's original etching plates, which had been presumed missing for a quarter of a century, had suddenly reappeared—in the possession of a lawyer from Greenville, North Carolina. The 75 plates, including the one shown above (an original print from which appears on page 147) went on display in the North Carolina Museum of Art in Raleigh. Fewer than a half-dozen other plates are known to exist, all held in European collections.

Robert Lee Humber, the owner, had secretly purchased the copper plates in 1938 from Alvin-Beaumont, a French collector who had last exhibited them in a New York gallery in 1930. Although most of the plates are worn and have been reworked since Rembrandt's time, they are highly prized as collector's items. Humber did not reveal the purchase price—in 1930 the collection was insured for half a million dollars—nor did he explain why he concealed his treasure in a New York warehouse for 18 years. It was not mere coincidence, however, that he finally broke silence in 1956—the 350th anniversary of Rembrandt's birth.

Chronology: Artists of Rembrandt's Era

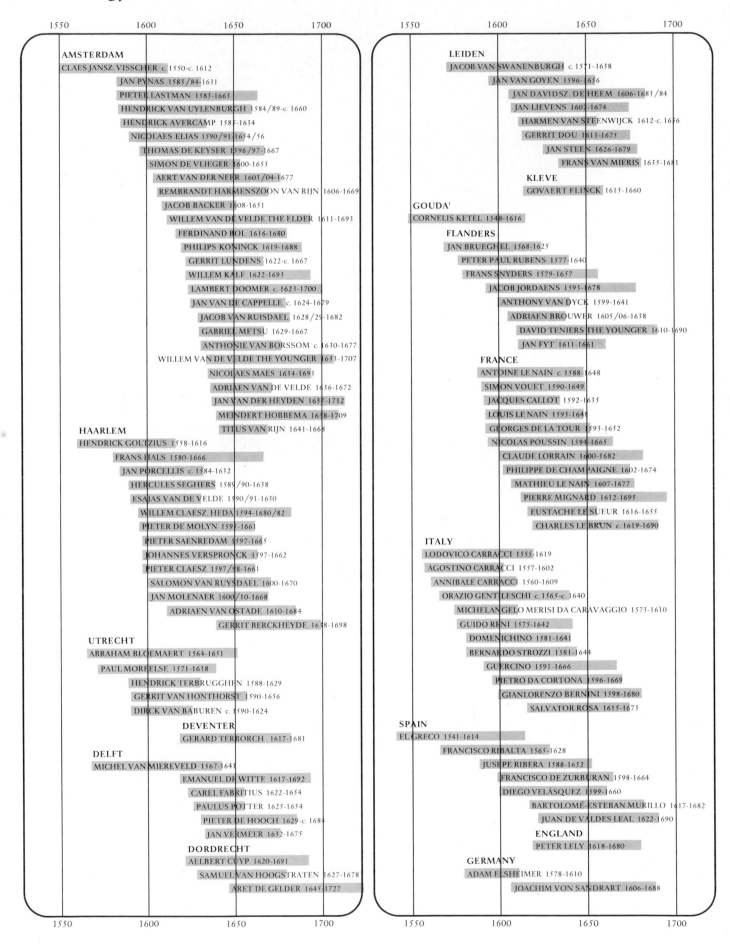

	1550	1600	1650	1700

AMSTERDAM
CLAES JANSZ. VISSCHER c. 1550-c. 1612
JAN PYNAS 1583/84-1631
PIETER LASTMAN 1583-1663
HENDRICK VAN UYLENBURGH 1584/89-c. 1660
HENDRICK AVERCAMP 1585-1634
NICOLAES ELIAS 1590/91-1654/56
THOMAS DE KEYSER 1596/97-1667
SIMON DE VLIEGER 1600-1653
AERT VAN DER NEER 1603/04-1677
REMBRANDT HARMENSZOON VAN RIJN 1606-1669
JACOB BACKER 1608-1651
WILLEM VAN DE VELDE THE ELDER 1611-1693
FERDINAND BOL 1616-1680
PHILIPS KONINCK 1619-1688
GERRIT LUNDENS 1622-c. 1667
WILLEM KALF 1622-1693
LAMBERT DOOMER c. 1623-1700
JAN VAN DE CAPPELLE c. 1624-1679
JACOB VAN RUISDAEL 1628/29-1682
GABRIEL METSU 1629-1667
ANTHONIE VAN BORSSOM c. 1630-1677
WILLEM VAN DE VELDE THE YOUNGER 1633-1707
NICOLAES MAES 1634-1693
ADRIAEN VAN DE VELDE 1636-1672
JAN VAN DER HEYDEN 1637-1712
MEINDERT HOBBEMA 1638-1709
TITUS VAN RIJN 1641-1668

HAARLEM
HENDRICK GOLTZIUS 1558-1616
FRANS HALS 1580-1666
JAN PORCELLIS c. 1584-1632
HERCULES SEGHERS 1589/90-1638
ESAJAS VAN DE VELDE 1590/91-1630
WILLEM CLAESZ. HEDA 1594-1680/82
PIETER DE MOLYN 1595-1661
PIETER SAENREDAM 1597-1665
JOHANNES VERSPRONCK 1597-1662
PIETER CLAESZ 1597/98-1661
SALOMON VAN RUYSDAEL 1600-1670
JAN MOLENAER 1600/10-1668
ADRIAEN VAN OSTADE 1610-1684
GERRIT BERCKHEYDE 1638-1698

UTRECHT
ABRAHAM BLOEMAERT 1564-1651
PAUL MOREELSE 1571-1638
HENDRICK TERBRUGGHEN 1588-1629
GERRIT VAN HONTHORST 1590-1656
DIRCK VAN BABUREN c. 1590-1624

DEVENTER
GERARD TERBORCH 1617-1681

DELFT
MICHEL VAN MIEREVELD 1567-1641
EMANUEL DE WITTE 1617-1692
CAREL FABRITIUS 1622-1654
PAULUS POTTER 1625-1654
PIETER DE HOOCH 1629-c. 1684
JAN VERMEER 1632-1675

DORDRECHT
AELBERT CUYP 1620-1691
SAMUEL VAN HOOGSTRATEN 1627-1678
ARET DE GELDER 1645-1727

LEIDEN
JACOB VAN SWANENBURGH c. 1571-1638
JAN VAN GOYEN 1596-1656
JAN DAVIDSZ. DE HEEM 1606-1683/84
JAN LIEVENS 1607-1674
HARMEN VAN STEENWIJCK 1612-c. 1656
GERRIT DOU 1613-1675
JAN STEEN 1626-1679
FRANS VAN MIERIS 1635-1681

KLEVE
GOVAERT FLINCK 1615-1660

GOUDA'
CORNELIS KETEL 1548-1616

FLANDERS
JAN BRUEGHEL 1568-1625
PETER PAUL RUBENS 1577-1640
FRANS SNYDERS 1579-1657
JACOB JORDAENS 1593-1678
ANTHONY VAN DYCK 1599-1641
ADRIAEN BROUWER 1605/06-1638
DAVID TENIERS THE YOUNGER 1610-1690
JAN FYT 1611-1661

FRANCE
ANTOINE LE NAIN c. 1588-1648
SIMON VOUET 1590-1649
JACQUES CALLOT 1592-1635
LOUIS LE NAIN 1593-1648
GEORGES DE LA TOUR 1593-1652
NICOLAS POUSSIN 1594-1665
CLAUDE LORRAIN 1600-1682
PHILIPPE DE CHAMPAIGNE 1602-1674
MATHIEU LE NAIN 1607-1677
PIERRE MIGNARD 1612-1695
EUSTACHE LE SUEUR 1616-1655
CHARLES LE BRUN c. 1619-1690

ITALY
LODOVICO CARRACCI 1555-1619
AGOSTINO CARRACCI 1557-1602
ANNIBALE CARRACCI 1560-1609
ORAZIO GENTILESCHI c. 1565-c. 1640
MICHELANGELO MERISI DA CARAVAGGIO 1573-1610
GUIDO RENI 1575-1642
DOMENICHINO 1581-1641
BERNARDO STROZZI 1581-1644
GUERCINO 1591-1666
PIETRO DA CORTONA 1596-1669
GIANLORENZO BERNINI 1598-1680
SALVATOR ROSA 1615-1673

SPAIN
EL GRECO 1541-1614
FRANCISCO RIBALTA 1565-1628
JUSEPE RIBERA 1588-1652
FRANCISCO DE ZURBURAN 1598-1664
DIEGO VELÁSQUEZ 1599-1660
BARTOLOMÉ-ESTEBAN MURILLO 1617-1682
JUAN DE VALDES LEAL 1622-1690

ENGLAND
PETER LELY 1618-1680

GERMANY
ADAM ELSHEIMER 1578-1610
JOACHIM VON SANDRART 1606-1688

Rembrandt's predecessors, contemporaries and successors are grouped chronologically according to country. The bands correspond to the life-spans of the artists.

Bibliography *Paperback

Note: Since there is such a wealth of literature on Rembrandt, this is a selected list of material that the editors believe would be of most interest to the reader.

REMBRANDT—LIFE AND WORKS.

Bauch, Kurt, *Rembrandt Gemälde*. A catalogue raisonné of Rembrandt's paintings. Walter de Gruyter & Co., Berlin, 1966.

Benesch, Otto, *Rembrandt: Biographical and Critical Study*. Translated by James Emmons. Editions d'Art, Albert Skira: Zwemmer, 1957.
The Drawings of Rembrandt (6 vols.). Phaidon Press, 1954-1957.
Rembrandt as a Draughtsman. Phaidon Press, 1960.

Boon, K. G., *Rembrandt: The Complete Etchings*. Thames & Hudson, 1963.

Bredius, Abraham, *The Paintings of Rembrandt*. Phaidon-Verlag, Vienna, 1936.

Clark, Kenneth, *Rembrandt and the Italian Renaissance*. John Murray, 1966.

Gerson, H., *Seven Letters by Rembrandt*. L.J.C. Boucher, The Hague, 1961. Translation and discussion of Rembrandt's brief correspondence with the secretary of the Prince of Orange about the Passion series he painted for the Prince. These are the only known letters by Rembrandt.

Goldscheider, Ludwig, *Rembrandt*. Phaidon Press, 1960.

Hind, Arthur M., *A catalogue of Rembrandt's Etching* (2 vols.), second edition. Methuen and Co., Ltd., 1923. *Rembrandt*. Oxford University Press, 1932.

Hofstede de Groot, Cornelis, *Die Urkunden über Rembrandt (1575-1721)*. Martinus Nijhoff, The Hague, 1906. Indispensable compilation of the documentary sources.

Landsberger, Franz, *Rembrandt, The Jews and the Bible*. Translated by Felix N. Gerson, The Jewish Publication Society of America, Philadelphia, Pennsylvania, 1946.

Münz, Ludwig, *The Etchings of Rembrandt* (2 vols.). Phaidon Press, 1952.
Rembrandt Harmenszoon Van Rijn. Harry N. Abrams, New York, 1954.

Rosenberg, Jakob, *Rembrandt: Life and Work* (revised edition).* Phaidon Press, 1964. The best monograph on Rembrandt's art and achievement.

Slive, Seymour, *Drawings of Rembrandt with a Selection of Drawings by His Pupils and Followers* (2 vols.).* Dover Publications, Inc., 1965.
Rembrandt and His Critics: 1630-1730. Martinus Nijhoff, The Hague, 1953.

Valentiner, W. R., *Die Handzeichnungen Rembrandts (Klassiker der Kunst)* (2 vols.). Deutsche Verlagsanstalt, Stuttgart, 1925. Not complete. A catalogue raisonné of Rembrandt's drawings. The third volume was never published.
Rembrandt and His Pupils.* The North Carolina Museum of Art, Raleigh, North Carolina, 1956.
Rembrandt and Spinoza. Phaidon Press, 1957.

Visser't Hooft, W. A., *Rembrandt and the Gospel*.* Translated by K. Gregor Smith. S.C.M. Press, 1957.

White, Christopher, *Rembrandt and his world* (new edition). Thames & Hudson, 1964. A readable biography emphasizing the artist's life rather than his work.

CULTURAL AND HISTORICAL BACKGROUND

Boxer, C. R., *The Dutch Seaborne Empire, 1600-1800*. Hutchinson & Co., Ltd. 1965.

Fremantle, Katharine, *The Baroque Town Hall of Amsterdam*. Haentjens Dekker & Gumbert, Utrecht, 1959.

Friedrich, Carl J., *The Age of the Baroque, 1610-1660*.* Harper & Brothers, 1952.

Geyl, Pieter, *The Netherlands in the Seventeenth Century*. Barnes & Noble, Inc., N.Y., Ernest Benn Limited, Part One, second edition, 1961; Part Two, 1963.

Renier, G. J., *The Dutch Nation*. G. Allen & Unwin, Ltd., 1944.

Zumthor, Paul, *Daily Life in Rembrandt's Holland*. Translated by Simon Watson Taylor. Weidenfeld & Nicolson, 1962. First-rate social history.

ART—HISTORICAL BACKGROUND

Bergström, Ingvar, *Dutch Still-Life Painting in the Seventeenth Century*. Translated by Christina Hedström and Gerald Taylor. Faber & Faber, 1956. A thorough treatment of this phase of Dutch art.

Friedländer, Max J., *On Art and Connoisseurship*. Caniver, 1960.

Leymarie, Jean, *Dutch Painting*. Translated by Stuart Gilbert. Éditions d'Art, Albert Skira: Zwemmer, 1956.

Lumsden, E. S., *The Art of Etching*.* Dover Publications, Inc., 1962.

Nicolson, Benedict, *Hendrick Terbrugghen*. Percy Lund, Humphries & Co. Ltd., 1958.

Rosenberg, Jakob, *Great Draughtsmen from Pisanello to Picasso*. Harvard University Press, Cambridge, Massachusetts, 1959.

Rosenberg, Jakob, Seymour Slive and E. H. Ter Kuile, *Dutch Art and Architecture: 1600 to 1800*. The Pelican History of Art Series, Penguin Books, 1966.

Stechow, Wolfgang, *Dutch Landscape Painting of the Seventeenth Century*. Phaidon Press, 1966. An excellent, comprehensive survey.

Van Gelder, J. G., *Dutch Drawings and Prints*. Harry N. Abrams, Inc., New York, 1959.

Picture Credits

The sources for the illustrations in this book appear below. Credits for pictures from left to right are separated by semicolons, from top to bottom by dashes.

COVER:
Heinz Zinram
END PAPERS:
By permission of the Trustees of the Chatsworth Settlement

INTRODUCTORY ESSAY: 6—John R. Freeman by courtesy of the Trustees of the British Museum, London. 8—John R. Freeman by courtesy of the Trustees of the British Museum, London (4). 9—Scala. 10—Eric Schaal. 11—Dresden, Gemaeldegalerie photo. 12—Derek Bayes—Erich Lessing from Magnum; © The Frick Collection, New York. 13—National Gallery of Art, Washington, D.C. photo; Erich Lessing from Magnum—Henry Ely, Aix-en-Provence; Heinz Zinram. 14, 15—National Gallery, London photo.
CHAPTER 1: 16—Foto Blauel. 20—Maps by Rafael Palacios. 21—Courtesy Leiden University. 22—Herzog Anton Ulrich Museum, Brunswick photo. 23—Hein de Bouter. 25—© Rijksmuseum, Amsterdam—Giraudon. 26, 27—Campongara. 28—National Gallery, London photo—© Rijksmuseum, Amsterdam (3). 29—Harry Redl. 30, 31—Scala. 32, 33—Harry Redl; Marzari—Staatliche Museen, Berlin, Gemaeldegalerie photo. 34, 35—Foto Blauel.
CHAPTER 2: 36—© Rijksmuseum, Amsterdam. 40—The Metropolitan Museum of Art photo—© University of Oxford, Ashmolean Museum. 43—Hein de Bouter. 44—John R. Freeman by courtesy of the Trustees of the British Museum, London. 47—National Gallery, London photo. 49—Heinz Zinram courtesy the Barber Institute of Fine Arts, University of Birmingham, England. 50—© Rijksmuseum, Amsterdam. 51—Walter Steinkopf. 52—Foto Blauel—Derek Bayes. 53—The Pierpont Morgan Library photo. 54—Erich Lessing from Magnum. 55—Derek Bayes. 56—Derek Bayes. 57—Eric Schaal. 58—Derek Bayes by permission of the Trustees of the Chatsworth Settlement. 59—Derek Bayes.
CHAPTER 3: 60—Staatliche Museen, Berlin photo. 62, 63—Kryn Taconis. 66—No credit. 68—Staatliche Kunstsammlungen, Weimar photo. 69—Robert Morton. 71—Fogg Art Museum photo; John R. Freeman by courtesy of the Trustees of the British Museum, London. 73—© Rijksmuseum, Amsterdam. 74—© Rijksmuseum, Amsterdam. 75-77—Scala. 78-80—Hein de Bouter. 81—Frans Hals Museum, Haarlem. 82-87—© Rijksmuseum, Amsterdam.
CHAPTER 4: 88—Heinz Zinram. 90—Courtesy the New York Public Library, *Fron-*

tispiece from *Historische Beschrjvinghe van Amsterdam,* Jacob van Meurs, 1663. 91—© Rijksmuseum, Amsterdam (2). 92—Museum Boymans van Beuningen, Rotterdam photo. 93—© Rijksmuseum, Amsterdam on loan from the Royal Society of Antiquarians, Amsterdam. 95—© Rijksmuseum, Amsterdam. 97—Erich Lessing from Magnum. 98, 99—Derek Bayes by permission of the Trustees of the Chatsworth Settlement—By courtesy of the Trustees of the British Museum, London. 100—Robert S. Crandall—Bibliothèque Nationale, Paris. 101—Robert Lackenbach from Black Star. 102, 103—Herzog Anton Ulrich Museum, Brunswick photo.
CHAPTER 5: 104—Scala. 107—Erich Lessing from Magnum. 111—© Rijksmuseum, Amsterdam. 114, 115—Hein de Bouter. 117—National Gallery, London photo. 118, 119—Karel Neubert; Dmitri Kessel. 120—Eric Schaal. 121—The Metropolitan Museum of Art photo. 122, 123—© The Frick Collection, New York. 124—Scala. 125—The Metropolitan Museum of Art photo. 126, 127—National Museum, Stockholm photo. 128, 129—Staatliche Graphische Sammlung, Munich photo; National Museum, Stockholm photo. 130, 131—© Rijksmuseum, Amsterdam.
CHAPTER 6: 132—Lichtbeeldeninstituut, Amsterdam photo. 136—Municipal Archives, Amsterdam—John R. Freeman by courtesy of the Trustees of the British Museum, London. 140—John R. Freeman by courtesy of the Trustees of the British Museum, London—Eric Schaal. 143—Robert S. Crandall. 144, 145—The Metropolitan Museum of Art photos. 146—© Rijksmuseum, Amsterdam—© Rijksmuseum, Amsterdam; By courtesy of the Trustees of the British Museum, London. 147—© Rijksmuseum, Amsterdam—Robert S. Crandall. 148, 149—Robert S. Crandall. 150-153—© Rijksmuseum, Amsterdam. 154-157—Robert S. Crandall.
CHAPTER 7: 158—Cliché Musées Nationaux. 161—By courtesy of the Trustees of the British Museum, London. 164—Teylers Museum, Haarlem photo—Gemeente Musea, Amsterdam photo. 167—Gemeente Musea, Amsterdam photo. 169-171—Robert Lackenbach from Black Star. 172, 173—Cliché Musées Nationaux; Eric Schaal. 174, 175—Mauritshuis, The Hague photo. 176—Karel Neubert. 177—Dmitri Kessel. 178, 179—Karel Neubert. 180—The Metropolitan Museum of Art photo. 181—Bruce Roberts from Rapho Guillumette courtesy of Dr. and Mrs. Robert Lee Humber, Greenville, North Carolina on loan to North Carolina Museum of Art, Raleigh, North Carolina.

Acknowledgments

For their help in the production of this book the author and editors wish to thank the following people and institutions: Fedja Anzelewski, Staatliche Museen, West Berlin; Director Erwin M. Auer and Georg Kugler, Kunsthistorisches Museum, Vienna; Catherine Bélenger, Services des Rélations Extérieures, Musée du Louvre; Baroness G. Bentinck, Switzerland; Justus Bier, Director, The North Carolina Museum of Art; Madame Adeline Cacan, Conservateur du Musée du Petit Palais, Paris; Harriet Cooper, Deanna Cross, The Metropolitan Museum of Art; Prof. Jonkheer J. De Graeff, Oegstgeest; Department of Prints and Drawings, The British Museum; Department of Prints and Drawings, The National Gallery; Sylviane d'Origny, Chargée du Service de Documentation de Photographies au Cabinet des Dessins, Musée du Louvre; Miss Y. M. De Vrij, Associate Professor, Utrecht University; Pontus Grate, Deputy Keeper, National Museum of Fine Arts, Stockholm; Madame Guynet-Péchadre, Conservateur, Service Photographique, Musée du Louvre; H. W. Hamel, Municipal Museum, Amsterdam; Historisch Museum de Waag, Amsterdam; Dr. and Mrs. Robert Lee Humber, North Carolina; Caroline Karpinski, Assistant Curator, Print Room, The Metropolitan Museum of Art; Wilhelm Köhler, Staatliche Museen, West Berlin; T. Koot, General Secretary, Miss B. Stokhuyzen, Miss C. Vierveyzer, Rijksmuseum, Amsterdam; Director Walter Koschatzky and Renate Antonio, Graphische Sammlung Albertina, Vienna; A. Lutsenburg Maas, University Library, Leiden; Municipal Archives, The Hague; Museum Fodor, Amsterdam; Hans Heinrich Richter, Deutsche Fotothek, Dresden; Rijksprentenkabinet, Amsterdam; Haldor Soehner, Director, Bayerische Staatsgemaeldesammlungen, Munich; State Archives, Haarlem; State Archives, The Hague; Stichting Lichtbeeldeninstituut, Amsterdam; Th. H.J.D. Van Beerendonk, Curator, Museum "Het Rembrandt-Huis," Amsterdam; J. H. Van Borssum Buisman, Curator, Teyler's Stichting, Haarlem; A. Van Der Vaart, Administrator, Mauritshuis, The Hague; I. H. Van Eeghen, Municipal Archives, Amsterdam; Jonkheer Six Van Hillegom, Amsterdam; Miss A. J. Visser, Miss B.R.M. De Neeve, Museum Boymans van Beuningen, Rotterdam; D. Vollenga, Frans Hals-Museum, Haarlem; H. F. Wijnman, Amsterdam; Ben F. Williams, General Curator, The North Carolina Museum of Art; Leon Wilson, Associate Editor in Charge, Publications Department, The Metropolitan Museum of Art.

Index

Index (continued)

Finito di stampare nel mese di aprile 1971 presso le Officine Grafiche Arnoldo Mondadori - Verona - Printed in Italy